CAPTAIN JAMES T. SUTHERLAND

The Grand Old Man of Hockey

The Battle for the Original Hockey Hall of Fame

Recognized by hockey legend Arthur ("Art") Ross in the Roll of Honor as the founder of the International Hockey Hall of Fame, now the Original Hockey Hall of Fame, Captain James T. Sutherland is also a member of the other Hockey Hall of Fame in Toronto, recognized as a prime supporter of hockey in its formative years, and a champion of the OHA and CAHA.

Roll of Honour

Captain James T. Sutherland

One of the
Veterans of Canadian Hockey
and Founder of

The International Hockey Hall of Fame

Were there one pedestal in the International Hockey Hall of Fame to be occupied by one person who pioneered Hockey and then gave a lifetime of devotion and work to the Sport, that person would be

Captain James T. Sutherland

Born in Kingston, Ontario, October 10th 1870, Jim Sutherland played hockey in the first organized league of which there is record. The teams consisted of Queen's University, the Royal Military College, the Kingstons and the Athletics. He played "Point," a defense position, on the last named Club. Queen's won the championship, defeating the Athletics 3-0 in the final game.

Later, Captain Sutherland organized the Frontenacs, which under his management won numerous junior and intermediate titles in the Ontario Hockey Championship series. He became President of the Ontario Hockey Association and of the Canadian Amateur Hockey Association, and has been elected a life member of both. During World War One, he served four years with the Canadian Forces Overseas.

Captain James T. Sutherland well may be called the "Father of Hockey". He has devoted 64 years to the betterment of the Sport, and it is quite understandable that in recent years he has devoted his complete time to the Hockey Hall of Fame, which through his efforts was located in his native Kingston, Ontario, where it will be a lasting Memorial to this grand Sportsman and Gentleman.

Contributed by
Arthur H. Ross
Vice-President and Manager
Boston Bruins N.H.L. Hockey Club
Boston, Mass. U.S.A.
1949

CAPTAIN JAMES T. SUTHERLAND

The Grand Old Man of Hockey

The Battle for the Original Hockey Hall of Fame

J.W. (Bill) Fitsell

Foreword by Edward R. Grenda

QUARRY HERITAGE

BOOKS

Dedicated to the author's home team:
Barbara Anne, Carol Anne, Diane,
Jo-Ann, Gay Willann and Jan.

ACKNOWLEDGEMENTS

Captain Sutherland left a lasting legacy of his love of hockey and the City of Kingston. As historian for the International Hockey Hall of Fame and Museum, which he founded, I was privileged to organize, collate, and record the vast collection of clippings, articles, letters, and photographs compiled during more than 50 years. To President Mark Potter and colleagues, I am indebted for the ongoing opportunity to retain and study and write about the record of this remarkable man.

I am thankful also for the valuable information and insights offered by librarians and archivists from Kingston to Ottawa and Montreal. I owe a debt of gratitude to members of the Society for International Hockey Research, which was formed at the Kingston shrine in 1991 with 17 members and has grown to 600 history buffs around the world.

Key to the complete story of hockey's birthplace and the selection of Kingston as the site for the Hall of Fame was the contribution of Earl Zukerman, sports information officer for McGill University, who generously made available original correspondence between principals in Montreal and Halifax.

Special thanks must go to friend and colleague Ed Grenda, who wrote the foreword and provided his editorial skills and advice on the manuscript.

Last, but not least, I'm especially grateful to Bob Hilderley, publisher of Quarry Heritage Books, whose passion for the game he still plays shows in words and pictures. His dedication to publishing hockey and Kingston lore reflects the passion that "Hockey's Captain" exuded throughout his life.

Cataloguing in Publication Data is available.
ISBN: 978-1-55082-374-5

Edited by Bob Hilderley.
Designed and typeset by Laura Brady and Susan Hannah.
Photographs courtesy J.W. (Bill) Fitsell and the Original Hockey Hall of Fame. Cover portrait courtesy Hockey Hall of Fame / C. McDiarmid / Cartophilium.

Printed and bound in Canada.

Published by Quarry Heritage Books, an imprint of Quarry Press Inc, PO Box 1061, Kingston, Ontario K7L 4Y5 www.quarrypress.com

CONTENTS

From 1965 to 2012, the Original Hockey Hall of Fame was housed in this building next to the Memorial Centre arena in Kingston, Ontario. Selected exhibits from the collection will be on display at the Invista Centre arena until the hall moves to a new home in downtown Kingston. Note the square puck monument to the left.

FOREWORD

One of the most intriguing elements in sports history is the pervasive obscurity, if not mystery, enveloping the origins of a sport, especially those considered to be major in scope, character and popularity – notable lack of relevant documentation and other forms of empirical evidence has largely contributed to this deficiency. In the absence of the accumulation of critical evidence for accounts of the origins of these sports, many individuals who exhibit a disinclination to undertake the required pain-staking research resort to creating accounts of origin which derive either from hometown boosterism, wish fantasies, personal geographical preferences, or business opportunities. Much of this is false history or the manufacturing of a myth with little or no connection with reality.

Without a substantial backdrop of appropriate historical research, each sport has individuals who develop their own "creation myths," which is taken as gospel by many in the general population. This has largely been the case with baseball, football, and hockey.

In this book, Bill Fitsell, the doyen of hockey historians, has set his sights on the idea of hockey's origins and the consequence it has for an accurate understanding of the game's character and development. For Fitsell, this book is a labour of love. He is persistent. His work in this area is the fruit of a meticulous 50-year endeavour of undertaking extensive research, the contemplation of the implications of this research, and discussions with fellow hockey historians.

Fitsell adopts a three-pronged approach in this book. He deals with the origins debate as it has evolved; (b) the role of Captain James Sutherland, an early hockey administrator who sparked and continued the origins debate for several decades; and (c) the establishment of the International Hockey Hall of Fame in Kingston, Ontario, a project carried through by Captain Sutherland on the basis of his view on hockey's origins.

The hockey origins debate has a long pedigree. Often couched as "the birthplace of hockey" debate, arguments and claims about the game's origins in Canada started as early as 1893 when the Dominion Illustrated Monthly magazine asserted that hockey entered Ontario through Quebec. During the first 40 years of the 20th century, debates among hockey journalists and sports historians raged to determine which city should receive the highest hockey accolade: the designation of a city as hockey's birthplace. Montreal, Kingston, and Halifax were the most frequently mentioned cities in this connection. Through his position as the President of the Canadian Amateur Hockey Association and his unrelenting advocacy of Ontario, Captain Sutherland was able to persuade the NHL and the CAHA that hockey's birthplace was Kingston, Ontario. Doubtless this did not sit well among hockey organizers in Montreal and Halifax. What was especially significant in this debate was the reliance on hearsay and personal experience rather than solid empirical research. There was little reliable data or research that could be adduced to illuminate the dark areas of this issue.

This book has a highly original and innovative character in the sense that it is the first extensive biographical portrait of Captain James Sutherland, whose contributions to hockey's development and status as a notable cultural component in Canadian society. Captain Sutherland was an indefatigable advocate of hockey's speed, grace, and its rough and tumble character. Most importantly, he valued outstanding playing abilities of hockey players. It is this factor that prompted Captain Sutherland to propose a Hall of Fame to honour those players and officials for their high standard performances. By combining his belief that Kingston was hockey's birthplace and his zeal to recognize excellence in playing abilities, Sutherland was successful in having the hockey powers at that time accept Kingston as the home of the International Hockey Hall of Fame in the early 1940s. Although he was flawed as an historian, he stressed that history of the game is crucial in preserving its significant moments and laying the groundwork for the future. We are in Bill Fitsell's debt for his biographical portraiture on one of hockey's early builders.

Using his comments on Captain Sutherland's life as a departure point, Fitsell proceeds to trace the checkered history of the International Hockey Hall of Fame from the 1940s to the present. Because of financial difficulties experienced by the City of Kingston during the 1940s and 1950s and the exhausted patience of the NHL to have a structure built in Kingston, the NHL decided to abandon Kingston and built its own Hall of Fame in Toronto during the mid-1950s. However, a Kingston Hall continued to operate – or to struggle – on its own for the next 50 years.

This book fills a huge void in hockey's history in the twentieth century and emphasizes the role that Captain Sutherland played in this context. Again we are in Bill Fitsell's debt for the manner in which he has illuminated a part of hockey's history about which very little is known or recorded.

EDWARD R. GRENDA
Honorary President
Society for International Hockey Research

HOCKEY'S BATTLES OFF THE ICE

"Capt. James T. Sutherland conceived the idea of an international hockey hall of fame...to be erected in a place he believed as the real point of origin of hockey—Kingston." Clarence S. Campbell, NHL President at Hockey Hall of Fame Induction Dinner, Toronto, 1974.

Canadians seem to have an inalienable right to talk hockey 12 months a year. Whether the topic is local stars or NHL heroes, last night's match, or next year's Stanley Cup favourites, many Canadians are keen to join the Hot Stove League Debating Society – 24/7. Three perennial topics have been the origins of hockey, the birthplace of the game, and the best home for a hockey hall of fame.

1. Three Great Debates

What is hockey? That is the question I set out to answer in my previous book, *How Hockey Happened*. Few Canadians think they need to ask themselves this question. Most are convinced they know what hockey is. They are also quite aware of what the game means to them. But few Canadians have heard about the origins of the game – where it came from, how it started, and what contributed to its makeup?

Challenged by the question of hockey's genesis,

students of the game might turn to newspaper archives, encyclopedias, and the Internet for help, finding there a mountain of information, much of it equivocal, some of it conflicting, a lot of it flawed because of inadequate research. In the *New York Times* a reporter admitted in 1947: "Origins of few sports are so surrounded in mystery as those of ice hockey." *Merit Students Encyclopedia* (1967) doesn't offer much more help: "The origin of ice hockey is obscure."

Like Canada itself, hockey is made up of a peculiar mosaic of northern European 'immigrant' and indigenous North American customs. That may be why it means so much to Canadians. Hockey is who we are.

The *Sports Dictionary* on the Internet offers another tack on this the question in an entry on the origins of North America's four premier sports by examining their inventors:

Inventor of Basketball: James Naismith
Inventor of Football: Walter Camp
Inventor of Baseball: Abner Doubleday
Inventor of Hockey: J.G.A. Creighton

Creighton certainly deserves credit for organizing under one set of rudimentary rules the various stick and ball games being played on the ice in the 1870s, but hockey wasn't born in a blinding flash of his genius, as was basketball in the imagination of Canadian James Naismith in the 1890s. "Hockey was no brain-child conceived in the night and put into practice the next day," McGill University official E.M. Orlick wrote in the *McGill News* (1943). "The question is not when the game of field hockey, hoquet, hurling or shinney started, but rather when and where did hurley or shinney develop into the game of ice hockey as we know it today?" As celebrated historian A.M. Lower commented in *Canada: A Nation* (1948), "There is no proof as to where and how hockey originated, but its chief ancestors seem to have been shinny and field hockey."

Despite many authoritative comments on the origins of hockey, the ultimate truth is that hockey, the great Canadian ice game, was not born, invented, or created -- it just happened. Hockey evolved from several pastimes played on both land and ice in different parts of the northern hemisphere and developed into the thrilling and sometimes brutal sport that most of the world knows today. As Robert Giddens remarked in his book, *Ice Hockey*, "No game or sport comes into being from a standing start. There are always traces of old sport in the new."

To discover hockey's roots, I inspected its various predecessors, such games as hurling in Ireland, shinty in Scotland, bandy and field hockey in England, as well as shinny, ricket, and ice polo in North America. Add in Native American lacrosse and shinny with some rugby-football and an ice-skating pastime and what happens is hockey. Like Canada itself, hockey is made up of a peculiar mosaic of northern European 'immigrant' and indigenous North American customs. That may be why it means so much to Canadians. Hockey is who we are.

As to where hockey was first played in Canada, Montreal, Quebec, Halifax, Nova Scotia, and Kingston, Ontario have been in the forefront of these debates. Additional claims for the honor have been submitted from Dartmouth and Windsor, Nova Scotia; Niagara, Ontario; Winnipeg, Manitoba, and Deline, North West Territories. Even the well-deserved contentions of Ottawa, Ontario and Quebec City, Quebec were tossed into the verbal fray. Most of the isolated claims were found wanting. Few centres have been able to produce proof that initial reports of 19th century skirmishes on ice developed into a skein of evidence linked to today's game. There was just no connection or continuity.

Still, more than a hundred years later, this debate is very much alive. As a *The Globe and Mail* sports writer commented in 1941, "The argument about the birthplace of hockey will probably last forever." So true! In the new millennium, hardly a year passes without some community laying claim to be the "birthplace" of our national winter sport.

As a The Globe and Mail *sports writer commented in 1941, "The argument about the birthplace of hockey will probably last forever."*

Another hockey debate, lasting for almost as long, has been where to locate a hockey hall of fame. When the suggestion of having a hockey shrine was first proposed in 1940, Baz O'Meara at *The Montreal Daily Star* immediately mentioned three cities as a possible site for a hall. "Toronto isn't considered for a number of reasons," he stated in his column The Passing Sport Show. "Toronto came into hockey late, and while many good advocates up there could muster some notable reasons for its selection, it would undoubtedly be ruled out on the grounds that while its claims might be appealing, Montreal, Kingston, or even Ottawa have more substance in their demands." The Hall would naturally belong in the city that was the birthplace of the game – but that was not easy to determine.

The early debates were centred on Montreal and Kingston and then later on Halifax, but the Toronto rival ended up as the eventual home for the hockey shrine. Now, almost forgotten, is the Ontario city located halfway between Montreal and Toronto — Kingston — that led the debate for decades. The Limestone City was the home of a remarkable man, who carried the military title of "Captain" and provoked and promoted the longest-standing debate in the history of Canadian sport. The debate over where to locate a hall of fame opened the doors to a debate that rages to this day.

This is the story of the founding of the Original Hockey Hall of Fame and the Grand Old Man of Hockey, Captain James T. Sutherland, who argued, successfully at first but ultimately unsuccessfully, that Kingston was home to the first game of organized hockey in our nation and would make the ideal site for a hockey hall of fame.

Regardless of the birthplace of hockey, the game originated from the merger of a variety of European and North American aboriginal stick and ball games, including hurling, shinty, field hockey, bandy, gugahawat, and baggataway, or lacrosse, which means "Little Brother of War." Painting by E.C. Coates, 1859.

The Eighth Duke of Beaufort, K.G.

Explains how the game of

Ice Hockey was first called

"Bandy"

and was played in 1813-14

Bandy is also closely associated with ice hockey, as documented by Capt. James T. Sutherland and the Hockey Hall of Fame Committee in the 1940s. Organized bandy was first played in England as early as 1813.

A STICK USED IN
ONE OF THE FIRST GAMES OF HOCKEY IN ONTARIO
QUEEN'S VS R.M.C.
KINGSTON FEBRUARY 1888
PRESENTED TO
THE GENERAL ALUMNI ASSOCIATION
BY
A.B. CUNNINGHAM ESQ. ARTS '91

Montreal and Halifax have documented proof of the earliest organized hockey games, but Kingston has the oldest puck in captivity—thanks to Queen's University. First used in 1886 in the inaugural game between Queen's and RMC, this "square" puck was cut from a rubber lacrosse ball and propelled by field hockey sticks. Puck and stick are displayed at the Original Hockey Hall of Fame on loan from Queen's University Archives. Souvenir facsimiles are available at the gift shop.

The tricoloured Queen's University jersey from 1895, worn by team captain Guy Curtis, is the oldest hockey sweater on record, now displayed at the Original Hockey Hall of Fame. Other historic sweaters displayed at the Hall of Fame include the Kingston Frontenac's jersey from 1912. The team won the OHA Junior championship, coached by James Sutherland.

HOCKEY SWEATER
CA. 1912, KINGSTON FRONTENACS SENIOR HOCKEY CLUB. THE SWEATER IS MADE OF WOOL, AND HAS A POLO NECK. SWEATERS WERE DESIGNED TO MAKE THE TEAMS DISTINCTIVE ON THE ICE AND TO PROTECT THE PLAYER FROM COLD TEMPERATURES AND WINDS. GAMES AT THIS POINT IN HOCKEY'S HISTORY WERE PLAYED ON OUTDOOR RINKS.

Them's Fighting Words

These debates were characterized by their bellicose language, which is not surprising given that the game's written history is replete with attack metaphors -- "fighting, conquering, battling." Organized Canadian hockey was barely into its teens in 1894 when an anonymous Montreal newsman tagged the winter pastime as the country's "national sport." The official designation wasn't confirmed in law until exactly a century later—1994—when Ottawa parliamentarians, in a classic Canadian compromise, combined the ice sport with a field game and declared both as the country's two official national sports—winter and summer. The summer sport was lacrosse, a field game that grew out of the aboriginal activity of "baggataway," also known as "The Little Brother of War."

"Serious sport… is war minus the shooting," British author George Orwell declared in 1945 just after the Second World War came to an end. While tough-as-nails hockey players have been described as "soldiers" and "warriors," even "gladiators," and players who play injured give the game its "warrior ethic," this violent ice game involving sticks and blades and boards has not been seriously aligned with out-and-out carnage between warring nations. Hockey's "battles" have mainly been "wars of words," not fought on battlefields but in boardrooms and in the media. "Wanna start a fight? Talk about the birthplace of hockey, Josephine Matyas advises in her *TripAtlas*, 2011.

Former National Hockey League coach Donald S. Cherry, shortly after he broke into CBC's *Hockey Night in Canada* as a commentator, used the analogy in praising the diggers, muckers, and "lunch bucket brigade" of today's game. "Bob Nystrom is a real foot soldier," he told Stan Fischler of *GOAL* magazine in 1983. "If they are going to win they've got to have the infantry men to complement the aces."

In the midst of the 2010-11 debate over the NHL's attempts to control blindside head hits and the mounting number of concussions suffered by players, Rick Dudley, then general manager of the Buffalo Sabres, debated this issue with David Shoalts of *The Globe and Mail*. Dudley questioned how these violent acts could be legislated out of the game. There will always be injuries because of the nature of the game, he conceded, but added that there "is an element of hockey that appeals to a great number of people, that WAR-LIKE element."

In 1885, when hockey in Montreal was just a decade old, a McGill student jocularly reported on four "battles" that had been "fought" by the university team and tallied the casualties thusly: "Two defeats, killed none, wounded everyone." A repeat comparison with the ultimate clash of forces, appeared in 1896 when a team from Queen's College (now Queen's University) of Kingston, Ontario, traveled to Pittsburgh to introduce Canadian hockey to ice polo-playing Pennsylvanians. To promote the exhibition series, the U.S. locals welcomed the students as "Canada's defenders," and advertised the opening game on a block of ice as: "WAR BETWEEN UNITED STATES AND CANADA!" No blood was spilled as the more experienced invaders from the north easily triumphed over the Americans.

The **Globe** *and* **Mail** *headlined the game as "War on Ice." The red-coated gentleman cadets could not resist waving a banner that blared: "REMEMBER 1812!"*

Almost a century later, when cadets of Royal Military College of Canada "defended their national game from U.S. aggression" and fought West Point to a three-all tie in Kingston, *The Globe and Mail* headlined the game as "War on Ice." The red-coated gentleman cadets could not resist waving a banner that blared: "REMEMBER 1812!"

Another such verbal confrontation occurred in 1931 when the upstart American Hockey Association threatened to rival the well-established N.H.L. The main battleground was "The Windy City," where the upstart Chicago Shamrocks competed for fans with the Chicago Black Hawks. Canadian writer and illustrator Jimmy Thompson, in an article in *Maclean's* magazine, shouted "Hockey War?" and harnessed colourful military language to describe the dispute over signing certain players. "Forces are being quietly mobilized," he wrote. "There are rumblings of approaching conflict," and he hinted that hostilities might extend along "a wider front" before "terms of peace" could be dictated. Cooler and more peaceful heads prevailed.

A dozen years later in the midst of the Second World War, another debate caused observers and participants to revert to explosive words and aggressive metaphors printed in the daily press. It was all about "the birthplace of hockey," an argument that had been simmering for 40 years. The combatants armed themselves with such words as "civil war," and phrases like "turn my guns, "first shot in the battle," and "volley of shots," and hunkered down.

Trench warfare dominated the First World War of 1914-18, but during the 1939-1945 conflict there were more sudden, panzer-like attacks. However, the men who remained at home and got involved in "the hockey war," while men and women were overseas fighting and dying became entrenched in their arguments. There was very little give or take.

Military lingo still sparks today's hockey reports. During the Vancouver Winter Olympics of 2010, CTV play-by-play broadcaster Gord Miller paused during the Canada-Slovakia game to quote a Russian coach as saying: "To have success in a tournament like this your generals must become soldiers." Even in 2012, as Canadians planned to mark the bicentennial of the War of 1812, *Sportsnet Magazine* led off its NHL playoff feature with a pronouncement that "warfare" was on display. "Bodies were bludgeoned, blood was spilled, heavily armoured men charged one another, hacking and slashing one another in a frenzy to tear one another limb from limb," wrote Jordan Heath-Rawlings. It's as if everyone's thoughts were embroiled in a global conflagration. "People throw out words like WAR and BATTLE way too often when speaking about sports such as hockey," *Hockey Canada Captains*, complained.

During the Second World War, every rank from private and corporal to captains got into a verbal fire fight over hockey's birthplace. It was a fractious but not a vicious debate or a "battle royal." There were heated arguments, with only certain holds barred. The only explosions were caused by frustration, lack of ammunition or the ability to lay down a barrage of facts clearly enunciated, supported, and understood. In the Kingston camp, anchored by the Citadel of Upper Canada—Fort Henry and the Royal Military College (RMC) —was a retired army captain and a coterie of astute veterans of business and sports. On the Montreal front were academics of "Old McGill," who mustered forces behind a wall of scholarly evidence. And on the eastern sector, protected by the Halifax Citadel and three centuries of history, were wily Nova Scotian sportsmen, writers, and politicians who had a built-in hostility against centralist Canadians. Somehow, the Bluenosers managed to keep their powder dry throughout early shelling from the West.

Despite a later alliance of Montreal and Halifax forces, the early advantage in the puck war went to Kingston, all because of one-soldier and his indomitable spirit. Enter stage left—the man born to be "Captain"—James Sutherland—who refrained from using pugnacious words.

In his lifetime, Kingston advocate Captain James T. Sutherland had to contend only with the conflicting claims of Halifax and Montreal. Since the 1950s, a number of other communities, from Windsor, Nova Scotia to Deline, North West Territories, have claimed rights to the coveted title of the "Birthplace of Hockey.""

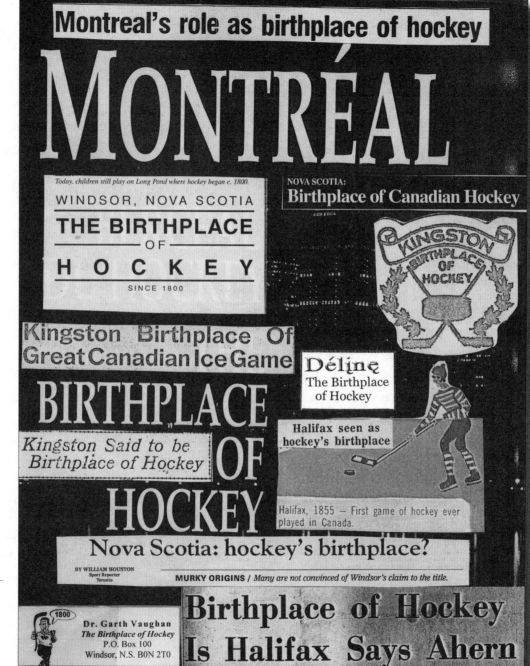

Montreal's role as birthplace of hockey

MONTRÉAL

Today, children still play on Long Pond where hockey began c. 1800.

WINDSOR, NOVA SCOTIA
THE BIRTHPLACE
OF
HOCKEY
SINCE 1800

NOVA SCOTIA:
Birthplace of Canadian Hockey

KINGSTON
BIRTHPLACE
OF
HOCKEY

Kingston Birthplace Of
Great Canadian Ice Game

Déline
The Birthplace
of Hockey

BIRTHPLACE

Kingston Said to be
Birthplace of Hockey

OF

Halifax seen as
hockey's birthplace

HOCKEY

Halifax, 1855 — First game of hockey ever
played in Canada.

Nova Scotia: hockey's birthplace?

BY WILLIAM HOUSTON
Sport Reporter
Toronto

MURKY ORIGINS / Many are not convinced of Windsor's claim to the title.

1800
Dr. Garth Vaughan
The Birthplace of Hockey
P.O. Box 100
Windsor, N.S. B0N 2T0

Birthplace of Hockey
Is Halifax Says Ahern

1842
December
S M T W T F S
1 2 3
4 5 6 7 8 9 10
11 12 13 14 15 16 17
18 19 20 21 22 23 24
25 26 27 28 29 30 31

1843
January
S M T W T F S
1 2 3 4 5 6 7
8 9 10 11 12 13 14
15 16 17 18 19 20 21
22 23 24 25 26 27 28
29 30 31

Arthur Henry Freeling, age 23

On the 14th October died my uncle Sir James Lyon, Colonel of the 24th Regiment, having a wife and 6 Children to lament him; how thankful I ought to be that my Father is not taken away from us and ourselves left to the precarious assistance & charity of friends & relations —

November.

Passes with no event of any moment to mark it —

December

Ordered on the 12th to Toronto to report on the road between the Fort & new Barracks at that place — Sleighed up in Stage of the 12th Toronto night of the 13th — at Mess with Story — 15th at 16th Mr. Maitland's (daughter Kingston) and be 18th (B. Arey) them to return to B___ see of Tor. many games at Rackets. I was delighted with my visit, the pleasure of which was enhanced by the cordiality my old friends received me.

with the 21st I was by the hospitable people Barron's House — and had

Rosedale, residence of Sheriff W. B. Jarvis

January — 1843 —

My Diary has now lived 3 years and a half — I myself am still spared, a living instance of God's mercy, while so many of my Relations are dying around me — Sl ___ permitted to finish this year? It ___ that I dare hardly ask ___ not fit to die. ___ ___ and ___ & Mother ___ be, at all ___ be happy; I hope I may ___ ted —

___ with Airey a & M. Hand drag (2 of my horses & his) to Napanee to bring into Kingston (B= & Mr. Maitland (sister to the Sampsons) and Miss Winslow distance 28 miles — started at 10, at Napanee at 1/2 past 1 — dined at Napanee, left at 4 came back by 1/2 past 7, having had a very pleasant drive — altho' the snow roads were rather heavy.

24th Drove Mr. Sampson, B. Maitland & wife, to Napanee on their way to Toronto — 4 Horses as before. Airey and myself driving —

Began to skate this year, improved quickly and had great fun at hockey on the Ice —

Began to skate this year, improved quickly on the Ice — had great fun at hockey on

While stationed in Kingston, 23-year-old Lieutenant Arthur Freeling (later Sir Arthur Freeling) recorded in his diary the first mention of hockey on the ice in eastern Canada: "Began to skate this year, improved quickly and had great fun at hockey on the Ice."

Dartmouth lakes near Halifax in the 1860s was a beehive of sports activities in the winter. Author Thomas Raddall, in his book Halifax: Warden of the North *(1948), claimed that "Ice hockey, Canada's national game, began on the Dartmouth Lakes in the eighteenth century." Halifax joined the battle over the birthplace of hockey and the home for the hockey hall of fame.*

Gunners of A and B Batteries of the Canadian artillery line-up with horses and sleighs on Kingston harbour ice behind Fort Frontenac. On the same site, British soldiers maintained a rink and played field hockey on the ice, as did military men in Montreal and Halifax.

When the National and American hockey leagues clashed in a verbal dispute in the 1930s, Canada's leading magazine, Maclean's, described it as a "Hockey War." Capt. Sutherland, with deep military roots, served in the First World War, but refrained from the use of "pugnacious words."

Maclean's Magazine, December 1, 1931   19

Hockey War?

By JIMMIE THOMPSON

The American Hockey League's claim to equality with the older National Hockey League is likely to result this year in a pitched battle of dollars and strategy

Frank Calder, President of the National Hockey League.

Tom Shaughnessy, Manager of the Chicago Shamrocks.

WAR—and I do not mean in Manchuria!

Right in your own backyard—in Toronto, Montreal, Chicago and New York—forces are being quietly mobilized, money bags are being given thoughtful consideration, the war lords are going into conferences.

Will this year see the American Hockey League, so-called outlaw organization, attain major status after a titanic struggle for recognition by organized

on his shoulder, he pointed it out to the major, and walked across the street to get himself a job as manager of the Chicago Shamrocks in the American League.

Tom immediately set out to get a corner on hockey. Among the financial backers of the Shamrocks he found men heartily in sympathy with his plans to build up a club that would outdraw the major's N. H. L. team.

Pro hockey, the movies, and the modern

Cartoonists Dunn & Scaduto have fun at the expense of the claim that Kingston is the birthplace of hockey. British troops are alleged to have cleared the ice at Fort Frontenac Barracks and played a version of field hockey on the harbour ice in 1861. Other historians have claimed the Ontario city created the game as early as 1843 or 1855. However, the first organized game was not recorded in Kingston until 1886 when teams from Queen's University and Royal Military College squared off.

Hockey Night in Canada *commentator Don Cherry, who revered Capt. Sutherland's "distinguished presence" and hockey knowledge, plunks for his hometown of Kingston as the birthplace of the game. In the 1990s, Windsor, Nova Scotia, led by retired surgeon Garth Vaughan, joined the birthplace battle.*

"Jim Sutherland more than loved hockey—it was his life!" William (Bill) Cook, Star of the New York Rangers and Member of the Hockey Hall of Fame, Kingston, 1972.

HOCKEY COMES TO KINGSTON

(1870-1920)

1. THE BOY AND THE GAME

James (Jimmy) Sutherland was the consummate Canadian kid—bright, athletic, and a sterling exemplar to all. He was born three years after the creation of this nation, in a city once chosen as Canada's first capital. It happened October 10, 1870, the year that British troops were "mustered out" and a truly Canadian military force established. The place was Kingston, Ontario, strategically located at the confluence of Lake Ontario and the great St. Lawrence River, and appropriately tagged as the Heartbeat of Canadian History and Hockey's Hub.

Jimmy marched and skipped to the beat of his own drum and made his history in a venerable garrison city and naval port and far beyond its shores. He was the youngest son of a prize-winning cobbler with Scots-Irish roots, who made boots for troops at Old Fort Henry, the citadel of Upper Canada, and prize-winning shoes for new Canadians.

Residing over the Sutherland shoe store on the city's main thoroughfare—Princess Street—James Thomas Sutherland was in the centre of Kingston's playgrounds on land and water. "The boys…were a pugnacious lot," one of the city's first historians reminisced in 1906. "They were formed into different squads or cliques and were very clannish. When the cliques met there was generally a fracas."

Tall, sturdy, and articulate, young Jim could "hold his own" at any level. Nearly all his friends could swim and handle a boat, loved sleighing and "were quite at home" on skates on Kingston harbour ice. "They could cut the figure eight and other fancy figures, but 'shinny' was their delight. Crowds would be placed at the Shoal Tower (in front of City Hall) and Point Frederick (at today's Royal Military College) and fifty or more players on each side would be in the game."

This last quotation, from the pen of Kingston Captain Edwin Horsey (1837-1908), later augmented by two key words—would be cited decades later by Jimmy Sutherland and broadcast nationally. Then affectionately known as "Cap'n Jim," or "Captain James T.," honored as one of "the Fathers of Hockey," who rose to the game's highest offices, Sutherland quoted Horsey in supporting a claim to hockey's origin and the right to host the game's original shrine.

He inserted — "soldier" before "boys" and "first" before "delight."

In his youth in the 1880s, James Sutherland had little interest in the roots of hockey. Playing the game for sheer fun was his main concern. "When school was out after four o'clock and on Saturdays, Kingston harbour was covered for miles in every direction with crowds of eager players divided into various groups," he recalled at age 60. "A considerable amount of real, old fashioned 'shinny' was played but not by the military chaps." Military personnel, he indicated, were playing a more organized game—"hockey-on-the-ice," the field variety as learned in British schools. As early as 1863, the Imperial troops had their own skating rink on the ice near Tete du Pont barracks, now Fort Frontenac.

The son of a military father, James was only 15 when he volunteered for service with the Midland Regiment that was mobilized for the Riel Rebellion in Canada's North West Territory. Rejected as too young for service, he was accepted into Kingston's 14th Princess of Wales Own Rifles two years later and launched a 50-year military career.

In the interim, on Kingston's frozen waterfront, an event took place that forever established the city as one of the cradles of Canadian hockey. Students at Queen's

University challenged and defeated the gentleman cadets of Royal Military College in a hockey match on March 10, 1886. Played under rudimentary rules written on a single sheet of paper, the game featured 14 players—seven a side—wielding roller polo sticks to propel an octagonal rubber puck. It was the first match in a series of annual games that would become the longest intercollegiate rivalry in hockey history. In a city where only old-fashioned shinny had been played, the launch of the new game found a permanent place in the mind of 16-year-old Jimmy Sutherland.

As he left his "teens," another mind-stirring event took place in Sutherland's Kingston. In 1890, a group of prominent citizens with the support of the Richardson grain family erected a covered skating and curling rink on the campus of Queen's University. Having only experienced skating on natural ice of Kingston harbour or inland ponds, Jimmy, now addressed as "James," must have dreamt about how much fun it would be to glide or play the new game on a sheet of indoor ice unencumbered by snow or rough, cracked surfaces.

Hockey teams gained permission from the skaters and curlers to use the new indoor surface and a new era in the city's sporting experience began for young men and women. Now 20 years of age and sporting a moustache grown for a part as chorus member in the opera "Leo, the Royal Cadet," James participated in a skating race at the first indoor carnival. The same winter he made his debut as a point player (defence) for Kingston's inaugural non-college hockey team— "The Athletics." They played against Queen's, RMC, and "The Kingstons" in the city's first organized league in the first provincial hockey organization in the winter of 1890-1891. It was called "The Ontario Hockey Association," or "Union," a distinguished body that Sutherland was destined to lead.

Students at Queen's University challenged and defeated the gentleman cadets of Royal Military College in a hockey match on March 10, 1886.

The Queen's team continued to dominate Ontario senior hockey. To compete, the Athletics and the Kingstons combined to produce a stronger lineup. Jim Sutherland's hockey playing career was interrupted in 1892, when his father, Alexander (Sandy) Sutherland, died. The youngest of a family of eight, James Thomas, who had put knowledge gained at a Kingston business school into practice as a bookkeeper for a hardware store, joined his brother John Henry in the family business. This reduced his active playing career but not his love for the game. He had reached his majority and was now eligible to vote. Years later he would proudly recall that he cast his first vote for Kingston's favourite son, the country's first prime minister, Sir John A. Macdonald.

They played against Queen's, RMC, and "The Kingstons" in the city's first organized league in the first provincial hockey organization in the winter of 1890-1891.

Shoes and hockey, not necessarily in that order, were uppermost in his mind. Queen's tricoloured team reeled off three consecutive Ontario championships and took permanent hold of the Ontario Hockey Association's (OHA) first trophy, the Cosby Cup—which predated the Stanley Cup and rests today at the university. In 1894, Sutherland took on more responsibilities when he exchanged marriage vows with Ethel Mary Metcalfe—a union that would endure for six decades. In 1897, he was "front and centre" when a new name was introduced to Kingston hockey circles—"The Frontenacs." The team was named after the famous French count, who also gave his name to the county in which Kingston is located. Sutherland became the team timekeeper and later refereed games before being appointed manager or coach.

Selecting the best of city talent and coaching with the aid of a megaphone, Jim's Frontenacs battled their way to the finals of the OHA's new intermediate division in 1897. Kingston lost out to Berlin (Kitchener) but not before charges of professionalism were sounded but unproven in the press. "Simon pure" amateurs, who played for the love of the game, was a tenet he fervently supported. As the OHA proclaimed: "Sport should be pursued for its own sake, for when professionalism begins, true sport ends."

Two years later in 1899, Sutherland was back with a new intermediate class team (players rated between juniors and seniors). The Frontenacs rolled over Belleville and Peterborough and captured the Ontario championship by soundly defeating the Guelph Nationals in the final. Manager Sutherland, with his hair parted in the centre, his moustache groomed, and a neat cravat below a high Don Cherry-like collar posed proudly with the blue-and-white champions and the new John Ross Robertson Trophy, emblematic of the OHA Intermediate crown. Greater challenges and victories were ahead.

Queen's University and Royal Military College organized a hockey challenge match in 1886, which Captain Sutherland cited as proof that Kingston was the birthplace of organized hockey. This match is re-enacted each year, with the addition of a team from the Canadian Armed Forces Base, Petawawa.

For more than a century, the historic hockey game was played on the harbour ice in front of City Hall, but is now played on the artificial ice pad behind City Hall in Market Square.

Jim Sutherland tried unsuccessfully to enlist in the army as a teenager to fight in the Boer War, but settled for donning a military uniform in the 1890s to play a role in the Kingston operetta, "Leo The Royal Cadet." In this formal portrait, the young officer displayed the moustache that graced his countenance for the rest of his life.

James' parents, Margaret and Alexander (Sandy) Sutherland, established a custom shoemaking shop on lower Princess Street and produced prize-winning boots for soldiers and civilians. James followed in his father's footsteps, and by the time he was 21, he traveled as far away as Savannah, Georgia, and Florida on sales trips, accompanied by his brother on occasion. Salesman Sutherland liked nothing better than talking hockey on his sorties across Canada and into the southern United States.

Princess Street

> *Dedicated to the Memory of*
> *Corporal Edward Filson,*
> *Canadian Mounted Rifles,*
> *a native of Amherst Island, Ont.*
> *Killed in action near Belfast,*
> *South Africa,*
> *November 7th, 1900,*
> *aged 23 years.*

The Gallant Canadian Lad.

James Sutherland wrote this poem, excerpted here, on December 27th, 1900, dedicated to the memory of Corporal Edward Filson, Canadian Mounted Rifles, a Native of Amherst Island, Ont. killed in action near Belfast, South Africa, November 7th, 1900, aged 23 years.

He would go, they could not stop him, for he came of fighting stock;
Though his widow mother pleaded, he was firm as any rock.
Well he loved the patient woman who had nursed him on her breast,
Been quite blind to all his follies, but he loved his country best.
"I'll come home again," he told her, "I'll come home again, some day."

Laid his face to hers and kissed her, said good-bye, and marched away.
Stronger than the voice that pleaded, "Eddie, Eddie, stay at home,"
Was the shrill voice of the bugle and the deep voice of the drum;
Calling him all the day, calling to him in his dreams;
"Come Ned, come lad, come, come, come."

His face was like a maiden's face, so smooth it was and fair,
The laughter in his eyes of blue, the sunlight in his hair;
But a man's heart, true and noble, beat within this gallant lad;
And a strong right arm he boasted, did this hero, khaki clad.
Oh, the battlefield is gruesome, with its dying and its dead;
But 'twas to the field of battle that the drum and beagle led, --
Belfast – and the bullets bitting fiercely left and right,
And the gallant lad in khaki there in the thickest of the flight.
Fearful odds and none to help them, though the hot sun burns and stifles.
Gallant kinsmen of the north land; brave "Canadian Mounted Rifles."
You fought nobly, this we know, When you net the desperate foe,
But you fought as heroes die, this all the world doth know.

Where the fighting had been fiercest, as the sun sank crimson red,
Did they find the widow's laddie, with a bullet in his head;
And his smiling face turned upward, did he dream at last – who knows:
Of his far off home in Canada – his "Lady of the Snows."
While the setting sun gleamed sorrowfully upon those eyes of blue,
And his khaki coat laid gently o'er the heart so brave and true,
Stilled forever with death's coming, did there fall upon his ear
Music that he loved to list to – bugle call so high and clear –
Thrilling, stirring, sweeter, shriller, and the deep voice of the drum,
Calling to him through the shadows,
"Come Ned, come lad, come, come, come.

HOCKEY

by Farrell

James Sutherland read Arthur Farrell's Hockey: Canada's Royal Winter Game, *the first formal history of the game, with great interest, and soon followed Farrell in tracing back "the sport to its very birth."*

DIFFICULTIES OF A TRAVELING SALESMAN

No, this is not a prayer meeting. Just "Jimmy" Sutherland selling shoes by candlepower at the Kind Edw ard (Hotel).

2. CHAMPION OF AMATEUR HOCKEY

The turn of the century into the 1900s was a momentous time for "James T." who had dreamed about joining army ranks since he was 15. When Canadian veterans of the Boer War were welcomed back to Kingston, he was caught up in the spirit of pride and nationalism. He clipped and saved an article on a rising young British war correspondent, Winston Spencer Churchill, and wrote a 36-line poem, "The Gallant Canadian Lad," dedicated to a young corporal who died with the Canadian Mounted Rifles in South Africa: "He would go, they could not stop him, for he came of fighting stock; though his widow mother pleaded, he was firm as any rock." At age 30, these lines must have inspired him to join the Army Service Corps as a reserve officer.

Besides reading military manuals, Lieutenant Sutherland had the opportunity to peruse the first book ever published on the new Canadian pastime. Entitled *Hockey: Canada's Royal Winter Game*, it was written by Arthur Farrell, star forward of the Montreal Shamrocks, whose mother, Mary Meagher, was a native of Kingston. This history-making handbook gave a short history of the origin and development of "the game of games." The fact that it was not Farrell's intention "to trace back the sport to its very birth" must have struck a note with Kingston's Sutherland, for he was soon to provide his own view on where the game began.

Farrell's intention "to trace back the sport to its very birth" must have struck a note with Kingston's Sutherland, for he was soon to provide his own view on where the game began.

Despite his corps duties, the young militia officer continued his interest in the Frontenac Hockey Club and took them on a three-game exhibition jaunt to Pittsburgh, where Queen's teams had been drawing crowds of 4,000 to 5,000 fans. The Pennsylvanians, boosted by ex-patriot Canadians, were tough competitors by 1902, and the Kingston team was held to two 2-2 ties and lost the third by one goal. "Manager Sutherland was coaching his favourites in a loud voice and rushed up and down the sidelines with excitement," reported *The Pittsburgh Press*. In the second match the visitors were stymied by opposition goaltender Pinky Lamb, a Kingston native, who played the full game wearing his old Kingston Frontenac sweater instead of his Pittsburgh Athletic Club jersey. Sutherland could only smile—with pride and irony.

By this time, his success as a coach and his rich knowledge of the game attracted the attention of the Ontario Hockey Association, and in 1902-03 he was appointed convener for the eastern Ontario group.

Highly respected and tagged at age 30 as "The Grand Old Man of Hockey," Sutherland was recruited to referee games in the Quinte district and other parts of Ontario. "He was strict, thoroughly impartial and caught everything," said *The Daily British Whig* of Kingston in reporting a record 33 penalties called in a Lindsay-Peterborough playoff game in February, 1909.

Highly respected and tagged at age 30 as "The Grand Old Man of Hockey," Sutherland was recruited to referee games in the Quinte district and other parts of Ontario.

Referee Sutherland had become conversant with the press and aware of how to promote the game and his hometown. *The Whig* noted his "deep fondness for the great game," saluted him as "one of the poppas of hockey" and published a list of 14 stars developed by him. "He has not only an eye of faith that can pierce the gloom but has a voice that can soar like a trumpet blast." The sporting editor suggested he should have become an evangelist. A staunch Anglican, his Bible was a hockey rule book and his mission quite clear.

"The birthplace of hockey was Kingston," *The Daily British Whig* emphatically declared in 1903, and lauded Jim Sutherland without quoting him as the source. "Kingston not only produced many of the brightest lights amongst the public men of Canada, (e.g., Prime Minister Sir John A. Macdonald) but it also produced the game today that is conceded to be the national winter game of Canada." *The Toronto Star* picked up the story, broadcast it with Sutherland's name as "the originator," and the first shot in hockey's greatest battle had been fired.

It did not matter to him that the opposing newspaper, *The Kingston Daily News*, had published a report that stated the game was introduced to the Ontario city by Royal Military College's skilful players from Halifax. And no one pointed to the *Dominion Illustrated Monthly* magazine article of 1893 stating, "Hockey skated up into Ontario from the Province of Quebec." The Sutherland version was born, and like Topsy, the story grew and seeds were sewn for the great debate.

Sutherland had other matters on his mind in 1904. The popular sportsman and lieutenant resigned his commission in the militia and was presented with a gold ring and best wishes. He had accepted a position as traveling salesman with a shoe company that would take him to the eastern United States and as far south as Florida. The new vocation gave him an opportunity to talk about his favourite sport and its beginnings.

The Sutherland version was born, and like Topsy, the story grew and seeds were sewn for the great debate.

In 1905, *The British Whig* again credited Kingston as "the birthplace of Canadian hockey" in bewailing the fact that the old Ontario city "had turned out dozens of noted players but never retained them long." One future star for Frontenacs and Queen's seniors was rover Marty Walsh, who went on to lead the Ottawa Silver Seven to Stanley Cups in 1909 and 1911. He scored 10 goals in one Stanley Cup match. Other less notables had migrated in a different direction to New York and Pittsburgh. They did what Sutherland had done—gone south for financial opportunities.

Sutherland was unaware of a booklet published in 1905 by the Montreal Amateur Athletic Association (MAAA) that summarized in detail the city's early hockey history. However, the staunch supporter of amateur hockey and good sportsmanship undoubtedly would have agreed with the MAAA official's comment on the state of the game: "How different was the early game to those of the present day! The players were not armored like Knights of the Round Table period; neither were they earnest searchers after each other's gore. They played the puck, and gashed heads were ever accidental. Though the game has since become faster, perhaps, it has deteriorated in one respect—it has become rougher."

The Kingston claim lay dormant as the Sutherland traveled to the United States and talked shoes, if not hockey boots. In 1908, the debate over "The Beginning of Hockey" was revived by a sportsman, not in Montreal but in Toronto, where hockey had a belated start in 1888. H.J.P. Good, the sporting editor of *The Toronto News*, tipped the direction in favour of Montreal in an article in the *Canadian Courier* magazine. His source was R.F. Smith, a Montreal photographer, who first played for McGill in 1881.

Illustrated by photographs of the first McGill University team of that year, the article made an appeal for more research on the early history of the game. "The early records of cricket have been embodied in one volume and something similar might be done for sports of other kinds," Editor Good wrote without reference to Farrell's ice-breaking booklet on hockey. He argued that: "If this were undertaken now, before the present old generation passes away, much information could be secured which will otherwise pass away with these older men."

Then Good added the zinger: "Hockey flourished in Montreal ten years before it grew popular in any other part of Canada." Although the game had spread to Quebec City and Ottawa, in Kingston's case it was exactly true. Later research, however, revealed the first organized game was recorded in Montreal in 1875 and the initial Kingston game wasn't reported until March 1886.

Strangely enough, support for Montreal as the "Mecca" of hockey first came from the City of Kingston, where Queen's students had become the first challengers for the Stanley Cup.

Montreal, credited in print as "The Home of Hockey" as early as 1893, and the place where the first league (The Amateur Hockey Association of Canada) was formed in 1886, was confident but quiet in its historical position. After all, wasn't a Montreal team awarded the first Stanley Cup in 1893 and the Quebec metropolis was where sportsmen designed and built the first arena for hockey in 1899?

Strangely enough, support for Montreal as the "Mecca" of hockey first came from the City of Kingston, where Queen's students had become the first challengers for the Stanley Cup and fell before the vaunted Montreal Amateur Athletic Association in 1895 and to Ottawa in 1899. Days after Good's *Courier* revelation appeared, Major A.B. Cunningham, who played in the third Queen's-RMC

game in 1888, backed Montreal as the originator of Canadian hockey. Speaking at a complimentary banquet given the Ontario Hockey Association champion 14th Regiment team by city council, the Major showed off the stick that he used in 1888 and coolly maintained that hockey started in Montreal 10 years earlier.

James Sutherland, despite his great rapport with the press, was silent. He was too wrapped up in creating history on ice. Sutherland was just as strict as a manager/coach as he was as a referee. He allowed his hand-picked junior teams to celebrate their victories—under control. After a big win in Oshawa in 1910, he took the team to Toronto for a "blow-out." That term meant nothing alcoholic to drink. "Jim will not tolerate any of the boys being treated by the many enthusiastic hockey sports," an anonymous *Whig* sporting editor explained. "No booze or late hours for these youngsters is Jim's motto."

His beloved Frontenacs, headed by future Hall of Famer, Allan M. (Scotty) Davidson, won the Ontario junior crown in 1910, ending Stratford Midgets' three-year championship reign. Before the start of the next season, Sutherland's champs, with another future inductee, George T. Richardson as president, defeated Montreal A.A.A., the Quebec champions, and claimed "the championship of Canada."

"The Frontenacs have a team of seven sturdy men. Last year they won the championship--this year they'll win again!" chanted the team's rooters. The prophecy was correct. The well-drilled and managed team swept all but one game and was saluted with full-page spreads in the Kingston press. At a civic banquet, their leader was presented with a five-piece silver set to go with the gold watch of the previous season. As a token of gratitude for bringing honours to Kingston in a clean sport, he was also presented with a handsome rocking chair "to sit in when he was too old to get to the rink." However, he had no thoughts of retiring from his much beloved game.

The Toronto press, headed by W.A. (Billy) Hewitt, sports editor of *The Star*, took special notice. "Where do you dig up all these new players," he asked in print. The gregarious Sutherland had no trouble answering. "On January first, we just strolled down to the ponds on the outskirts of town, looked over the kids, with and without skates, most of them with shinneys, selected 30, cut them to 10, held another practice, picked out seven and here we are!" *The Toronto News* gave the "Father of the Frontenacs" a glowing tribute for his "splendid sportsmanship, and his clear vision in picking out players and forming them into teams."

The editor saluted him for fathering many of the rules in the OHA book. One of his innovations in the day when seven men played the full 60 minutes was to allow substitution for injured players. Sutherland introduced a change from two 30-minute periods to three 20-minute periods. And he proposed a constitutional amendment designating the point and cover point players as right defence and left defence.

---

*The **Toronto News** gave the "Father of the Frontenacs" a glowing tribute for his "splendid sportsmanship, and his clear vision in picking out players and forming them into teams."*

Sutherland had become as popular as his star players. During games, the Kingston Frontenac Rooters chanted the song from 1911:

Oh Jimmie Sutherland, Oh Jimmie Sutherland,
The greatest coach the country ever knew.

The OHA recognized him for other talents. Appointed to the executive in 1911, he was acclaimed as second vice-president in 1913. At the same time he was taking Kingston teams on exhibition tours of Detroit and Boston and spreading the word about The Limestone City as the "birthplace of hockey." Few sportsmen denounced the claim. Their thoughts were directed to more serious matters.

From the sparkle in his eye, James Sutherland appears to be enjoying his life as a traveling salesman, hockey coach, OHA executive, parent, and husband.

Most hockey teams in this era had young boys as team mascots. They were thought to bring good luck. One of the first to serve the honourary position was Captain Sutherland's son, James. He donned the blue and white colours of the famous Kingston Frontenacs and demonstrated his stickhandling and skating abilities before games.

Two years after Sutherland was involved in creating the "Frontenacs" hockey team, he led Kingston to its first OHA championship. The Captain's seven-man team rolled over all opposition in the new Intermediate division.

*Manager and coach Sutherland sits front and centre with his mascot son James Sutherland above,
as Kingston Frontenacs, OHA Junior champions of 1910-11, pose for noted photographer Henderson.
The powerful team was regarded as "Junior Champions of Canada."*

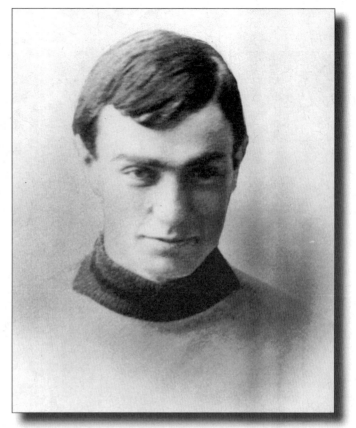

(Left) One of Sutherland's first hockey heroes was Marty Walsh, who jumped from Queen's University seniors to the famous Ottawa Senators and led the National Hockey Association in scoring.

(Right) When war was declared in 1914, Frontenac's great star George Taylor Richardson said: "That means me." Months later he died in action, and his old coach, Capt. Sutherland sought out his grave before returning to Canada in 1919.

(Left) Allan (Scotty) Davidson led Sutherland's Frontenacs to the Ontario-Quebec junior title and then captained the Toronto Arenas to the Stanley Cup in 1914. He joined the First Canadian Army Division and died in action in France in 1915, age 24.

(Right) Frontenac grad William (Bill) Osser Cook became captain of the New York Rangers in 1926 and won the Stanley Cup twice playing on the famous "Bread Line" with his brother Fred ("Bun") Cook and Frank Boucher.

GRAND OLD MAN OF HOCKEY

CAPTAIN JAMES T. SUTHERLAND

Who Originated and Secured Hockey's Hall of Fame For Kingston

Captain James T. Sutherland — known from coast to coast as "The Grand Old Man of Hockey", the man who has done more to make this country hockey-conscious than any other half dozen people in the game. A most ardent enthusiast, an old player with a colorful and sensational career on the ice, and a brilliant executive head, James T. is one of the best advertisements that the Limestone City ever had. Just say James T. Sutherland in any one of the nine privinces and you immediately conjure up the thoughts of Kingston and hockey.

To go fully into his career would call for all the skill of a professional biographer for the Captain has tried his hand at more important positions on executives and other angles of the hockey game than any other man alive or dead. Here are a few of the real highlights of his long and interesting career: a member of the Ontario Hockey Association since 1911; president of the I.H.A. in 1914 and 1915; president of the Canadian Amateur Hockey Association for four years, a distinction that has never been held by any other man. As if these honours aren't enough, he is the only life member of both the C.A.H.A. and the O.H.A.

When reminiscing Capt. James likes to recall the old Athletics team he played on in 1885 in a league composed of Queen's University, the Royal Military College and the Kingston Athletics. This league was in operation five years before the O.H.A. came into existence and is, as a matter of fact, the first hockey league the world ever knew. The Athletics were composed as follows: goal, J. Elliott; point, James T. Sutherland; cover-point, F. Roney; forwards, F. Rockwell, C. McCrae, C. Wilson, D. McRae, T. Parkins and J. Renton. Queen's and the

"JIM"

Athletics met in the finals and the Tricolor emerged victorious to the tune of 3-0. Those early days of hockey remain ever green in the memory of Capt. James Sutherland, as well they might.

Hats off to the gentleman who has guided the destinies of so many hockey enterprises successfully, one of the greatest living hockey authorities, Capt. James T. Sutherland.

3. THE DEADLIEST GAME

The First World War broke out in 1914, and the following year James Sutherland was promoted to first vice-president of hockey's major organization and appointed coach of the OHA East all-stars. With many of Sutherland's old Frontenacs marching off to army camps, he still had lots of fight left in him on the hockey front. He lashed out at the owners of Cleveland's new artificial ice rink for offering paid positions in return for hockey services. "This is Canada's game," he told *The Globe* of Toronto, "and it is not going to be degraded to make a few dollars for American rink promoters or their tools in this country."

"Sutherland sayings," at least in Kingston, became part of hockey's lore. "Come on boys, work hard on the line!" was one of his popular pleas during a game but appropriate for trench warfare. Another of his megaphone messages at the rink was: "All up and at it!"

Following in the blade marks of such illustrious Frontenac favourites as Walsh, Davidson, and Richardson—all future Hall of Famers—was a new name—Cook—destined to be hailed as the best forward ever to come out of The Limestone City. William Osser Cook, better known as "Bill," starred at age 18 for the Junior Frontenacs. In a playoff game in Belleville's "long, narrow rink," with 415 Kingston fans on board via a special train, the future New York Ranger star drew raves from The Daily British Whig: "Cook was always on the puck—backchecking was his forte." Despite a cut over one eye, the "hard, energetic player" scored a goal, batting a rebound off the goaltender's pads.

In 1916, at age 45, old soldier Sutherland volunteered for active service with the 149th Battalion mobilized in Kingston and at the same time became the newly-elected president of the OHA. Sutherland had become a favourite citizen of Kingston and a foremost hockey authority. As a journalist at *The Kingston Standard* explained in 1916, "In referring to Captain Jas. T. Sutherland, the President of the OHA, as 'Captain Jim,' we are not using a name of over familiarity; it is a title of honour."

Sutherland had become a favourite citizen of Kingston and a foremost hockey authority.

"The will to serve," commented Kingston sports columnist Mike Rodden years later, "was inherited from his Scottish ancestors and nothing could have deterred him from following the path of duty." According to family lore, the newly commissioned officer caught a severe head cold just before going overseas. He rejected the order of a senior officer to go on leave, doused a handkerchief with eucalyptus oil that cleared his breathing passageways and allowed him to rejoin his unit.

Although garbed in khaki and working in a military environment at Kingston's Barriefield camp, President Sutherland could not resist commenting on his favourite game. The consummate amateur, in a special communiqué, cautioned OHA teams about visiting Cleveland and Pittsburgh and such American cities that cater to the 'tourist' and professional amateur hockey players.

As the gravity of war becoming more intense, President Sutherland addressed a special New Year's message to "the great army of hockey players and officials" across Canada. With a touch of Churchillian oratory, he cited the great and urgent need for men "to come forward and rally to the defence of our common cause and strike a blow for liberty and justice that will re-echo around the world. There should be only one conclusion," he added, and that should be to exchange the stick and puck for a Ross rifle and bayonet. . . With every man doing his bit Canada will raise an army of brains and brawn from our hockey enthusiasts the like of which the world has never seen." And the proud old orator and referee added: "The whistle has sounded. Let every man play the greatest game of his life." His patriotic appeal paid dividends. Seven hundred and fifty former players and officials donned khaki. Sutherland urged other Canadians to make the total 1,100.

When the 149th Battalion moved overseas in September 1916 and was absorbed into the 95th Battalion, the Ontario Hockey Association, in annual session at Toronto's Temple Hotel, congratulated the absent Sutherland on his "unanimous re-election to office as president" and expressed appreciation of his long and valuable services to the national game." The resolution expressed hope for his "early and safe return to our councils."

"The whistle has sounded. Let every man play the greatest game of his life."

As German planes bombed London and blood flowed amidst the mud of France, Sutherland, serving as quartermaster of the casualty training battalion, turned his rallying cry to the world's deadliest game. "War is war and no man with good healthy red blood in his veins wishes to avoid the responsibility that the phrase 'on active service' entails, but when one looks around and sees the net result of one of these raids—the slaughter of innocent girls and women, a feeling of intense indignation that one cannot jump into a waiting aeroplane and go up after the swine, who can stoop to desecrate the holy Sabbath with such contemptible deeds." Now 47, the best active image the loyal officer could present was to hop on a dispatcher's motorcycle and pose for a photographer.

After five years of carnage, the war-to-end-all-wars concluded with an Armistice on November 11, 1918. On the date that the historic peace treaty was signed, Sutherland was in Paris. He took the opportunity to visit the gravesite of his beloved ex-Frontenac captain, Capt. George T. Richardson at Beleuil, France. Back in Britain, the surviving troop members turned their thoughts to more healthy activities, such as athletics. Captain Jim played a role as an official at a track and field meet in Hastings, Sussex. Hockey was still much in his mind, and he tried unsuccessfully to initiate competition for the troops at Manchester and London.

Captain Sutherland arrived home just in time to make a stirring speech on behalf of ex-army candidates at Kingston's newly-opened Great War Veterans' Hall. And appropriately, he was Jimmy-on-the-spot to lead the reorganization of his favoured Frontenacs. "Never in the history of Kingston were there so many young men anxious to get places on city hockey teams," noted *The British Whig* in December, 1919.

Despite the tragic loss of Corporal Scotty Davidson and Capt. Richardson in the killing fields of France and Belgium, Capt. Sutherland had to look no further for distinguished leadership on the ice than Bombardier Bill Cook, a battle-hardened veteran who had served with the Canadian Artillery in France and won a Military Medal fighting the Communists in northern Russia before gaining an honourable discharge.

Never in the history of Kingston were there so many young men anxious to get places on city hockey teams.

Cook, with support of Coach Sutherland, resumed his aggressive manner with the post war Frontenacs. His battling style was defended by sports writers in Kingston and Toronto. "Cook is a clean player and wears the King's decoration for bravery in action," commented *The Mail and Empire* of Toronto. It was the kind of calibre of spirited play that Sutherland promoted and praised for all his athletes. And it propelled Cook into a Hall of Fame career. No one was more proud than his old coach—the Captain.

*Lieutenant Sutherland (third row, fifth from the right) with the
149th Army Service Corps in training at Barriefield near Kingston.*

Motorcycle Dispatcher
Sutherland, during wartime service in England, had dreams of joining the action when he mounted a motorcycle for a photographer.

Zeppelin Damage
Capt. Sutherland (second from left) inspects damage caused by a German Zeppelin during a blitz on a hospital at Ramsgate, England, 1917.

*Ever the sportsman, Capt. Sutherland was among the officials at
a Canadian Army field day in England in 1918.*

A civilian for most of his 85 years, James T. Sutherland carried the title of "Captain" to his grave and was revered for creating a memorial to Canada's war dead. He proudly posed in his First World War khaki uniform.

PROLONGED ENGAGEMENT

(1920-1929)

1. CAPTAIN SUTHERLAND'S CLAIM

As Kingston moved into "The Roaring Twenties," the city's leading newspaper, *The Daily British Whig*, proclaimed: "Kingston has not received its due." Captain James Sutherland, who claimed he obtained the right to retain the rank of "Captain," moved to correct the alleged oversight about credit due his beloved hometown. He spoke out at every opportunity to raise the Limestone City to a new pinnacle in the sporting public's mind. *The Toronto Star* scooped up Sutherlandian tales about the game, including an anecdotal reminiscence about a Frontenac goaltender who deflected a puck into the crowd and learned later it broke the nose of his grandfather! In a more serious vein, Sutherland extolled Kingston as a producer of top-line players, citing the names of Dr. Charles Stewart, Flat Walsh, Johnnie Woodruff, Wally Elmer, Fred (Bun) Cook and his brother Bill, and eight others who had excelled in amateur and professional games.

Star sports editor Lou Marsh, the leading referee of the era, climbed on the Sutherland bandwagon: "Kingston claims its place in the sporting sun because the first authenticated games of organized hockey was played down on Kingston harbour," he proclaimed in December, 1924. "James T. Sutherland of Kingston says so and James should know."

In the same year, when Toronto sportsman George (Joe) King published and sold the first illustrated history of the Canadian game, the 174-page *Hockey Year Book* at $2 a copy, he gave Sutherland a place up front for an article entitled the "Origin of Hockey."

"I think it is generally admitted and has been substantially proven on many former occasions that the actual birthplace of organized hockey is the city of Kingston, in the year 1888."

"Whatever measure of merit the claims of other places may have,"said Sutherland, "I think it is generally admitted and has been substantially proven on many former occasions that the actual birthplace

of organized hockey is the city of Kingston, in the year 1888." He cited the Queen's-Royal Military College game played on the harbour ice, which actually started in 1886 and noted his own participation in the first city league.

In 1924, in a move that perpetuated the myth that Kingston was "the first hockey match on Canadian record," Queen's University opened its second indoor, natural ice arena. Built on Queen's campus, the frame and steel rink was named in memory of the late Dr. J.J. (Jock) Harty. The son of former Queen's chancellor Sir Sandford Fleming, Walter Fleming, who, played for the Tricolour in the 1888 game, faced off the puck as his Alma Mater met their old rivals, the cadets of RMC. The fine hand of Captain Sutherland could be seen in the indoor re-enactment and the historic publicity.

He repeated the birthplace claim in 1925 with a full-page *Whig* article entitled, "Hockey Heroes of Former Days Made Game Famous in Kingston." In another pronouncement, labelled "a splendid address," by the local media, he stressed the need for "clean sport." As Kingston Combines came within one goal of capturing the trophy he championed—the OHA Memorial Cup—while playing the Calgary Canadians in 1926, he urged the OHA to eliminate all heavy and unnecessary bodychecking on the forward line. *The Toronto Star* backed him in efforts to stop defencemen from "crashing into attacking forwards."

Sutherland's puck opinions reached national publications.

Sutherland's puck opinions reached national publications. *MacLean's* magazine, in an article entitled "A six letter word meaning the best game in the world," Toronto author Charles H. Good cited Sutherland as one of hockey's uncles, "if not the actual father" of the game. He wrote: "If the records are not all astray, [Sutherland] took part in the organization of the first ice hockey league the world ever saw." This was a claim that the Captain broadcast for years, but Montreal sources disproved this with evidence that the Quebec metropolis had formed the first league five years before Kingston's four-team group of 1891.

Nonplussed, Sutherland extolled the virtues of amateur hockey while praising the number of simon pures—from Hooley Smith to Happy Day and Lionel Conacher—who had "made good with a vengeance" in the National Hockey League. None rated more high praise than the Cook brothers, Bill and Bun, who starred in the Western league before brightening Broadway with the New York Rangers in 1926-27. "For real mad-brained hockey, deadly shooting right on the nets and for all-round sportsmanship the two brothers are hard to beat," exclaimed *The Kingston Whig*. "It is no wonder the Cook brothers have gained a large following." Coincidentally, one of the Rangers' first programs contained Sutherland's Kingston birthplace story.

Between trips made for a national firm to the United States, the intrepid salesman sold shoes and hockey, not necessarily in that order. A decade before it happened, he urged universal rules for all hockey and championed the founding of a Kingston Amateur Athletic Association, a movement popular in metropolitan centres. His steady advocacy on behalf of the game resulted in national honours. The Canadian Amateur Hockey Association, the national body that he represented on occasions at playoffs, made him a Life Member in 1928. He shared the honour with Winnipeg's Claude Robinson, a CAHA pioneer, and Montreal's W.M. Northey, the distinguished gentleman who helped establish the Allan Cup for senior championship honours. "Through his works in the interests of the amateur game he has won for himself the title of 'Father of Canadian Hockey.'"

"Through his works in the interests of the amateur game he has won for himself the title of 'Father of Canadian Hockey.'"

Honoured and revered, the popular gentleman turned to campaigning for his hometown and its hockey heritage. In 1928, he wrote a full-page article for *The Whig-Standard* entitled "Kingston—The Birthplace of Hockey." The next year, 1929, the prolific Sutherland wrote another extensive article headed, "Who put hockey on the map?" He modestly excluded himself from the list of dignitaries and shone the spotlight on such puck pioneers as Montreal's W.H. Northey and Toronto's William Hewitt.

2. MONTREAL'S CLAIM

The year 1929 saw the first major crack appear in Sutherland's claim that Kingston was the first home of hockey. In October, the American stock market collapsed and the economy went into a nose dive. Weeks later, as if somehow related to sports, the shock opened up a Pandora's box of evidence on hockey being played and developed in Montreal several years before the first games in the Limestone City. In November 1929, veteran Quebec sportsmen voiced opinions based on personal participation in games preceding Kingston's inaugural ice activities. Arthur E. Scott of Quebec City wrote to veteran Montreal sportsman W.E. Findlay and declared hockey was first played in the Ancient Capital in 1878-79 and listed the names of teammates. L.A. Vandette, secretary-treasurer of the Montreal Amateur Athletic Club, re-ignited the debate with a revelation printed in a brochure issued in 1905. The anonymous writer related how Montreal athletes seeking an equal game to lacrosse of summer and familiar with rugby football, and aware of field hockey rules, devised a new game—Canadian ice hockey—in the early 1880s. He named dates and officials and lineups of teams representing MAAA, Victorias, and McGill University.

In December, more supplementary evidence followed from Joseph W. Richards of Verdun, Quebec. He listed the names of seven players who lined up with the Montreal Victoria hockey club against Quebec City in 1881. He was secretary of the "Vics," a club he maintained was organized in the late 1870s. This pushed the game's birth date even further back from the Kingston genesis. Veteran Montreal and businessman and prominent sportsman W.E. Findlay, former secretary of the Victoria Hockey Club, elevated the debate with a comprehensive listing of the founding dates of various clubs: Victorias, Quebec, and McGill in the mid and late 1870s and Ottawa in the early 1880s.

Hockey's birthplace was in the Province of Quebec is a certainty.

"That ice hockey is Canada's national winter sport is admitted," he wrote. "That hockey's birthplace was in the Province of Quebec is a certainty, although from statements made…in Ontario and the West, the impression has been created…that hockey originated in Kingston about the year 1888." He followed with a list of 15 Montrealers, including J.G.A.Creighton, who, as hockey pioneers, were involved in the Victoria club. Several days later, J.J. Collins of Westmount claimed fellow McGill student A.P. Low and others created hockey in 1881 and cited the names of 13 players who participated in early games.

"These are only a few sidelights on the early days of ice hockey," replied *The Montreal Star* sports editor. "And it would be very interesting if some of those who were then identified with the game would take the trouble to give further information so that a true record could be made." The appeal paid off with a letter from a former Montrealer living in Toronto that was published in *The Star* on December 18, 1929. Walter C. Bonnell reported playing hockey in Montreal in 1875 and tipped the debate in a new direction. He claimed that officials of the Victoria Hockey Club of Montreal, a subsidiary of the Victoria Skating Club, ordered hockey gear from Halifax.

The Montreal Star, under the heading "HOCKEY PROBABLY PLAYED IN MARITIMES BEFORE IT CAME HERE, commented: "it opens up a new avenue of speculation by suggesting that sticks and pucks and rules were known in Halifax before they were known here." Haligonians were slow to respond, but the Montreal observation turned the discussion into a three-pronged debate—from which it would never recover. For example, *The Star* commented in December, 1929: "Every year brings new claims as to the origin of ice hockey from various parts of Canada."

3. HALIFAX'S CLAIM

Montreal's Baz O'Meara, who had been in the centre of the debate from Day One, kept the hockey pot boiling by advocating Halifax as the game's originator.

The Star's sports editor switched the focus to Canada's east coast by using a reference of the Kingstonian he described as "one of the landmarks of the OHA and its main historian." Sutherland had coupled Halifax with Kingston as places the Royal Canadian Regiment were based in the 1860s and tagged the soldiers as "originators of the game."

In 1937, O'Meara, noting that Halifax and Kingston had been "preening their plumes while they contended for the birthplace honour," discovered "evidence" that would put Montreal ahead. He published a story by veteran reader John T. Knox about four Irish immigrants who brought hurleys with them in 1836 and introduced a new ice game "and a new and interesting claim" to Montrealers. "It must have been a glorious type of scrimmaging," commented O'Meara. "No referees. That would appeal to many. The claim seems logical. Hurley is something like hockey only the ball is kept in the air not driven along the ice or ground as in field hockey." Knox failed to reveal the names of the Irish quartet. The revelation evoked little or no comment, but the chronicler would be heard from later.

Capt. Sutherland always had an answer to his detractors whether in Halifax or Montreal. It wasn't games of hockey that were played in Montreal…with Halifax shinny rules," he said at his stickhandling best. "However, these games…do not fill the bill as to where 'organized hockey' had its birthplace." And that, of course, in his mind, was Kingston.

"Kingston's claims are treated lightly in the harbour town (Dartmouth)," stated *The Halifax Mail*. "According to some veterans, but never verified, somebody from Nova Scotia went to Kingston and taught Kingstonians the game." The quip wasn't far from the truth. Another voice was heard from Arizona, where former Montrealer W.L. Murray, 74, a graduate of McGill, was alleged to have established "the first crude hockey called shinney." To which *The Halifax Mail* replied: "This was indeed news to Dartmouth old-timers who recalled playing the Canadian pastime on the town's beautiful lakes in the fifties and sixties."

The Murray and Knox reports provoked indignation among Maritime readers. Prince Edward Island native Elmer Ferguson of *The Montreal Herald* jumped into the fray in 1936. "As every good Maritimer knows hockey began down on the Dartmouth lakes near Halifax, played there by the palefaces in the sixties and long before by the Indians." He quoted veteran Nova Scotian sports writer James W. Power, whose statements were substantiated by former Haligonian William Gill of Boston. "The game was started in reality on the North West Arm, near Halifax," he said.

Hockey began down on the Dartmouth lakes near Halifax, played there by the palefaces in the sixties and long before by the Indians.

Despite the blast from the east, loyal Kingston protagonists wavered—just slightly in 1936. Fred Beaudry and Herb Hamilton, who shared *The Whig Standard* sports column, agreed: "Just about when we confidently thought that James T. Sutherland had convinced all and sundry that Kingston was the birthplace of hockey along comes *The Halifax Mail* to sneer at the Limestone City's claims." The Nova Scotia writers quoted a former RMC cadet living in Chester, Nova Scotia, who maintained he introduced the game to Kingston in the mid-1880s. The lineups in the hometown newspaper shows the military college had three skilful players from Nova Scotia while McColl acted as a goal judge.

The Beaudry-Hamilton duo was most prophetic when they expressed doubt if the question of hockey origin would ever be settled to the satisfaction of everyone. Pending "definite proof," they decided to string along with James T. These writers were succeeded by William J. Walshe, formerly of *The Toronto Mail*, who became Sutherland's chief supporter. The new Kingstonian gave the Captain two full columns on his favourite initiative. "Captain Sutherland's ambition today is to definitely establish Kingston as the home of organized hockey. He has worked hard on getting positive facts that the first league in history operated and while other claims may get more publicity—he will probably soon succeed in proving his beloved home city as the birthplace of hockey."

In the next decade, Sutherland would heighten his emphasis on the city "where organized hockey had its inception," and launch a campaign to create a hall of fame for hockey.

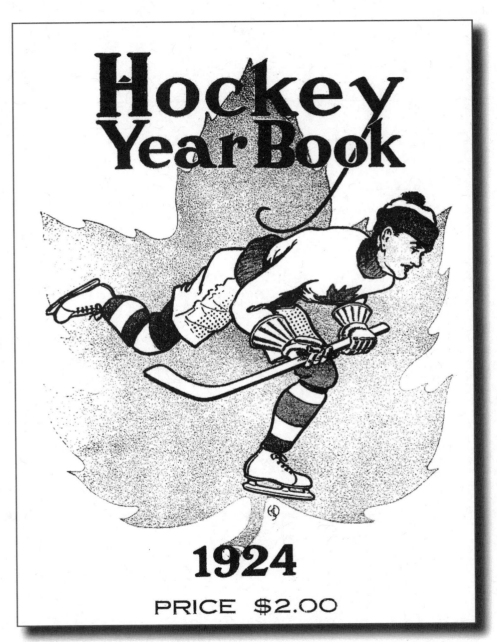

Hockey Year Book

1924

PRICE $2.00

Captain Sutherland's version of the birthplace of hockey was given prominence when it was featured in an article in The Hockey Year Book, *the first illustrated history of Canada's game. Published in 1924 by Joe King of Toronto (later of Kingston), the 174-page book provided an invaluable history of the amateur and professional game.*

ORIGIN OF HOCKEY

By Capt. James T. Sutherland

Past President Canadian Amateur Hockey Association;
Past President Ontario Hockey Association.

———

Historians are said to differ considerably over the place in which the great Cæsar first saw "the light of day," and similarly in respect to the birthplace of Canada's national winter sport. Hockey. There may be some who will claim sundry and divers places as being the authentic spot or locality.

Whatever measure of merit the claims of other places may have, I think it is generally admitted and has been substantially proven on many former occasions that the actual birthplace of organized hockey is the city of Kingston, in the year 1888.

The first actual game that we have any record of occurred in Capt. Dix's rink, which was located on the harbor in front of the city buildings, Kingston. This game was played between teams representing Queen's University and the Royal Military College. The players wore long white duck trousers, and used a set of sticks which had been borrowed from an eastern firm. said sticks being expressed back to the owners after the game. The rink, which was intended for skating purposes only, had a band stand erected in the centre of same, and when a player dashed up the ice he was greatly assisted in his attack by his agility to dodge around the band stand while en route. A solid rubber ball, which had been cut into a square, was utilized for the puck.

Following this introduction of what has since developed into Canada's greatest winter sport, a regularly organized hockey league was formed in Kingston. This league was composed of clubs from Queen's University, the Royal Military College, the "Athletics" and the "Kingstons." The final game was fought out between Queen's and Athletics, the former winning by 3 to 0. Col. A. B. Cunningham, K.C., W. F. Nickle, K.C., M.P.P., Col. Irvine, etc., were members of the champion team. The writer played the position of cover-point for the Athletics.

This league had a most successful career; but, with the organization of a provincial body, which has ever since been known as the Ontario Hockey Association, some two years later, the league naturally merged with the larger body and ceased to exist.

Like other hockey historians at the time, Captain Sutherland was more interested in the birthplace of the game rather than the evolution of the game, despite his use of a Darwinian title, "origin."

KINGSTON, ONT BIRTHPLACE OF HOCKEY

In 1928, Sutherland continued his campaign to recognize Kingston by writing a full-page article, "Kingston, Ont. Birthplace of Hockey," for The Whig-Standard.

Earliest Hockey Game on Record, as Distinguished From the Ancient Game of "Shinney", Played on Kingston Harbour Between the Royal Military College of Canada and the University—League of Four Teams Played Series in 1888, This Being the

Origin of Hockey
By Capt. James T. Sutherland
Past President Canadian Amateur Hockey Association;
Past President Ontario Hockey Association.

Historians are said to differ considerably over the place in which Caesar first saw the 'light of day', and similarly in respect to the birthplace of Canada's national winter sport, Hockey. There may be some who will claim sundry and divers places as being the authentic spot or locality.

Whatever measure of merit the claims of other places may have, I think it is generally admitted and has been substantially proven on many former occasions that the actual birthplace of organized is the city of Kingston, in the year 1888.

The first game that we have any record of occurred at Capt. Dix's rink, which is located on the harbor in front of the city buildings, Kingston. This game was played between teams representing Queen's University and Royal Military College. The players wore long white duck trousers, and used a set of sticks borrowed from an eastern firm, said sticks expressed back to the owner after the game. The rink, which was intended for skating purposes only, had a band stand erected in the centre of same, and when a player dashed up the ice he was greatly assisted in his attack by his agility to dodge around the band stand while en route. A rubber ball, which was cut into a square, was utilized for the puck.

Following this introduction of what has since become Canada's greatest winter sport, a regularly organized hockey league was formed in Kingston. This league was composed of teams from Queen's University, Royal Military College, the "Athletics" and the "Kingstons." The final game was fought out between Queen's and Athletics, the former winning 3 to 0. Col. A.B. Cunningham, K.C., W.F. Nickle, Col. Irvine, etc., were members of the champion team. The writer played the position of cover-point for the Athletics.

This league had a most successful career; but, with the organization of a provincial body, which has ever since been known as the Ontario Hockey Association, some two years later, the league naturally merged with the larger body and ceased to exist.

MCGILL UNIVERSITY FIRST HOCKEY TEAM 1881

McGill seniors posed for Notman photographers at the Crystal Palace Rink in what is believed to be the earliest hockey photograph. The first organized hockey game was played in Montreal.

Considered to be the founding father of organized hockey in Canada, J.G.A. Creighton moved from Halifax to Montreal, where he amalgamated the rules of Halifax and Montreal versions of the game into one "national" sport.

Hockey Probably Played In Maritimes Ere It Came Here

Walter C. Bonnell, Who Says Story of His Death Much Exaggerated, Remembers Sticks And Pucks Being Brought From Halifax

Montreal Star   Dec. 18, 1929 (p34)

In regard to the continued and diversified claims to the where and when ice hockey started, an old controversy received reopened by W. R. Findlay of this city, the following letter should be interesting. It not only backs up previous statements published in The Star about the time it was first played in Montreal, but it opens up a new avenue of speculation by suggesting that the sticks and pucks and rules were known in Halifax before they were known here.

The gentleman who wrote the letter is one who was considered dead by J. W. Richards, of Verdun, who wrote about old-time hockey about a week ago, but he says in the celebrated words of Mark Twain that Mr. Richards' statement is very much exaggerated. Here is his letter:

300 Avenue Road,
Toronto, Dec. 16, 1929.
Sporting Editor, Daily Star.

Mr. Harry G. Stewart a friend and a Montrealer, sent me the enclosed clipping of your issue dated Dec. 2, 1929, page 44, regarding the birth of hockey—ice hockey. I played two games of hockey, one in February and one in March in 1875 with the Victoria's. The Victoria Hockey Club was about one month old then. One game was at a place called "The Tank," the other was in the Victoria Skating Club, Drummond street, now immediately behind the Windsor Hotel not built in 1875. The other game was first at the Tank, an open air rink close to St. Lawrence Main street and north of Sherbrooke street, two or more blocks, and east of St. Lawrence street.

LACROSSE ON ICE

Before the Victoria Hockey Club started in December, 1874, lacrosse was played on ice, seven on each side or team. Opposing players, played in pairs all over the ice, only two clubs

[...] was scored. The game was the most furious speed game The Great Almighty's humans ever indulged in. The last was in the Victoria Rink and the ball the same size as used in the field game, only hollow for air to enter with one small air hole to prevent speed and long carriage. At this the ball persistently found its way to windows and gas jet globes, making loss and being a danger to players and spectators from falling glass. Glass was on the ice and everywhere. The directors of the Victoria Skating Club met and decided no more lacrosse in the Victoria Skating Club's covered rink. Lacrosse was banned or "canned" for all time, and then hockey came into use sometime early in February, 1875.

FROM HALIFAX

Charles Torrance, the president of the Victoria Skating Club, and, I think, Col. Fred. Henshaw, ordered hockey sticks from Halifax, Nova Scotia as well as rules, and pucks, and any credit is due to these two gentlemen and sportsmen who formed the Victoria Hockey Club, really a subsidiary of the Victoria Skating Club which I was a member of from 1873 to 1876. I returned from boarding school in 1873 from England. Some United States citizens were trying to persuade me that football with the oval ball originated in the United States, when touring through there three months ago, they wilted when I informed them I played rugby as a boy in England at school in 1870, '71, '72, and in '73, '74, '75 in Montreal when Harvard came to Montreal to play McGill and McGill went to Harvard College. Teams were scarce in the United States at those dates. Montreal sportsmen in my day encouraged games and races always for exercise and pastime, never for individual gain by their arms and legs.

In a letter to the editor of The Montreal Star *on December 18, 1929, W.R. Findlay presented proof that he played organized hockey with the Victoria Hockey Team in December 1874.*

'TIMES HAVE CHANGED'

JOHN T. KNOX, Montreal octogenarian who says his father was among a group of men originating the game of ice hockey more than 100 years ago, and who played the game himself as a boy long before 1879, when the first hockey game was formerly thought to have taken place, is shown above examining a modern skate and glove. When Mr. Knox, 84, played hockey, they used old wooden runners with long knee boots and there was no such thing as a gauntlet. *Gazette photo (copyright reserved)*

Montreal Octogenarian Claims Hockey Invented 104 Years Ago

An 80-year-old Montrealer, John T. Knox, threw a monkey wrench into the birthplace race when he maintained Montreal's ice game developed from the Irish field game of hurling.

By
JOHN QUINPOOL

"*Chain Lakes, Dartmouth, Nova Scotia, in 1828, are reputed the scene of the first hockey in Canada.*"
—John W. (Quinpool) Regan, author of First Things in Acadia. Halifax, Nova Scotia, 1936.

Historian John W. Regan was the first to broadcast Nova Scotia's claim to hockey fame in the 300-page book, First Things in Acadia, *in 1936. Seven years later he joined a civic committee supporting Halifax's birthplace claim and rights to a hockey hall of fame.*

CIVIL WAR

(1930-1943)

"When the World War has been won, Canadian officials perhaps will devote themselves to trying to end the Civil War in the Dominion over the who, when and where of ice hockey." — Frank G. Menke, **Encyclopedia of Sports, 1943**

1. NO CAPITULATION

Back in Kingston as 1930 arrived, Captain Sutherland, who had dominated the debate until the Montreal revelations surfaced, seemingly ignored such claims. The enterprising Kingston native kept selling shoes and promoting pucks, particularly one version of the game's origin. He turned to his loyal, hometown paper and pontificated on how the game was introduced in Kingston by British soldiers, who turned field hockey and polo into hockey. "The Royal Canadian Rifles at Tete-du-Pont barracks away back in the sixties,'" he said, "formed the advanced guard for what became Canada's great national game."

No longer directly connected to a Kingston hockey club, Sutherland kept a close eye on local affairs and local officials' attempts to fill vacant executive positions. "It would be a tragedy (for Kingston) to drop out of the OHA. where organized hockey had its inception," he said in a letter to the sports editor of *The Whig-Standard* in December 1931.

"There is no greater storehouse of hockey information than Jim Sutherland — 'Old Man Hockey' — Baz O'Meara wrote in **The Montreal Star** *in 1934.*

The press noted his absence from the game. "If the same interest was taken in the welfare of the Kingston Frontenacs as shown in Belleville, they would return to the public eye as was the case some years ago when Jim Sutherland and company guided the destinies of Kingston hockey," charged *The Belleville Intelligencer*.

"There is no greater storehouse of hockey information than Jim Sutherland—'Old Man Hockey'—Baz O'Meara wrote in *The Montreal Star* in 1934. When the OHA. was accused of being "dictatorial," Sutherland rose to its defence and lauded colleague William A. Hewitt, a man whose support he would retain until death.

Other authors entered the fray, including Frank G. Menke, a noted American sports historian. In 1930, the New York based newspaperman published the *All-Sports Record Book*, embracing a history of all major sports. Under "Hockey—Its History," he claimed hockey was derived from baggataway, the old Indian game that became lacrosse and was soon straightened out by Canadian readers. Critics also jumped on him for repeating the claim that "the first real ice hockey game of which there is any record" was played in Kingston in 1888. Menke's five pages of hastily compiled history would face further revisions as the hockey debate unfolded.

Pioneer player R.F. (Dick) Smith, a commercial photographer in Montreal, claimed he drew up the first rules with the help of a fellow McGill student W. F. Robertson and played a nine-a-side game in 1879. He sent his hand-written report to Menke and enclosed a photograph of the first McGill team taken at Montreal's Crystal Rink in 1881 and a picture of medals he won at three winter carnivals in the city. "Previous to this a game without rules of any kind was played in the Victoria Skating Rink by teams of about 15 on each side," he added. Subsequent findings would prove his figures and dates inaccurate.

The first "literary" look at the game's early roots was presented in *Down the Ice*, written in 1934 by noted hockey play-by-play broadcaster Foster Hewitt, who produced books with the help of Toronto writer Henry Roxborough. One of the contributors was none other than James T. Sutherland, and "The Early Days of Ice Hockey" section led off with his claim of the Royal Canadian Rifles clearing the snow from the ice in Kingston harbour and playing a game in 1867. "For more than a decade, following the year of Canada's Confederation, ice hockey was void of rule and reason," he said, "it was but a vehicle of enjoyment for good-natured mobs of club-swingers." Prominently displayed was a sketch of the hand-hewn field hockey type stick used by Queen's University players against Royal Military College.

The Kingston story had taken on even more stature months before the Hewitt publication. Queen's alumnus Colonel Lennox Irving (Arts 1886) published a letter in *The Queen's Review* pointing to what he believed was "the first game of hockey in Ontario" against RMC in March 1886. The student periodical followed up with news of the presentation of the puck to the university. The octagonal shaped disc, cut down from a lacrosse ball, was presented by Irving, who scored the one and only goal. "The battered old puck…will be an invaluable addition to Queen's athletic treasures," said the *Review*. This oldest known puck has rested in a special display at the university and at the International Hockey Hall of Fame and Museum in Kingston, along with the original pages of two magazines describing the March 10, 1886 action, all entwined with Queen's Tricolour ribbon.

This oldest known puck has rested in a special display at the university and at the International Hockey Hall of Fame and Museum in Kingston.

The early happenings of Canadian hockey also elicited comments and queries from other American writers. The esteemed *Literary Digest* of New York credited Lord Stanley with introducing the game to Canada. To which *The Ottawa Journal* retorted: "The above, of course, is all nonsense. Ice hockey is of Canadian origin."

James A. Burchard of the *New York World-Telegram* asked: "How ancient is hockey? How did it start? There are a half a dozen rival versions concerning the birth of hockey," he noted, listing Montreal, Kingston, Ottawa, and Truro, Nova Scotia, "where goals were seven miles apart!" Canadian artist Jimmy Thompson turned the queries into a syndicated cartoon acknowledging all the claimants and requesting more insights.

The Canadian birthplace opinion was put on record quickly. In the 1936 book, *From Rattlesnake Hunt to Hockey*, a sporting history of the Brampton, Ontario area, author William Perkins Bull stated: "While the games from which hockey developed have been played by many older nations, the Canadians have most of the credit for perfecting this sport to a unique degree of swiftness and skill."

Montreal moved to the front of the pack when D.A.L. MacDonald of *The Gazette* stated emphatically: "The very game of hockey in fact had its beginnings in McGill. Hockey was played there in the early seventies and two McGill graduates drew up the first rules. They were both footballers with the result they incorporated the onside pass into the ice game."

Sutherland, the astute old coach, knowing that the best defence is a good offence, returned fire: "These persons are evidently quite sincere in advancing their claims. However, if organized hockey did come into existence in the various places and at the various dates that they claim, many of us may be pardoned if we asked them to explain just what has become of these sundry original organizations." Published in *The Whig*, the story was erroneously headed: "First Hockey in Kingston in Eighties." He stroked out the last word, inserted "Sixties," and filed it with his collection of scrapbook clippings.

The McGill Daily joined the fray with a 1934 article by former sports editor S.L. Janikun entitled "Hockey Under the Microscope." As its source, it cited a *Montreal Standard* story of the previous year, which plunked for R.F. Smith as the student who drew up the first rules in 1879. That article appeared under a heading that could well stand forever: "The Everlasting Story of Where and When Hockey Started." Support for Montreal came from W.M. Gladish, a Central Press Canadian sports writer. He maintained that "Old McGill" had been playing the game for 54 years. Sutherland took issue and reviewed the whole debate. "So much for the origin of hockey," he said without giving an inch. "Here in Kingston we claim…without contradiction that the birthplace of organized hockey is the old Limestone City."

2. BOOST FROM BASEBALL

A quarter century of debate over the place where hockey was first played produced skirmishes among the combatants, mostly verbal shots exchanged at long range. Halifax, Kingston, and Montreal supplied most of the ammunition. Come 1939, with real war clouds hovering over Europe, the Canadian hockey infighting intensified—all because of the actions by another sporting community in a neighbouring country.

The major baseball leagues of the United States of America celebrated the centenary of the national pastime in 1938 and a year later, June 12, 1939, established the National Baseball Hall of Fame at Cooperstown, New York. Two months later Great Britain declared war on Nazi Germany and Canada followed, but the number one hockey topic refused to go away. "Hall of Fame" joined "Birthplace of Hockey" among the pundits' language. Questions arose as to where to place a hall of fame?"

Old-time hockey, like baseball, suffers from the lack of authoritative history.

In January 1940, Montreal's chief protagonist, Baz O'Meara, summed up the situation: "Old-time hockey, like baseball, suffers from the lack of authoritative history. There is so much obscurity about its beginnings, too little known of its early history, its great games, great personalities of the past." He offered the names of NHL president Frank Calder, Stanley Cup trustee William Foran, and James Sutherland, "whose vigorous assertions that hockey started in Kingston always wins him a wide audience wherever he holds forth on his favourite subject."

The Montreal sports editor praised Sutherland for another reason: getting legislation that allowed players who signed professional contracts to be reinstated as amateurs after a one-year absence. "He had mingled with pro hockey players for many years. He had found them pretty good citizens. He liked their ways. He regretted that all amateurs who turned professional could not make the grade. So he wanted a way for them to retrace their steps to be retained for hockey."

Baseball's hall of fame opened and the first immortals were inducted with much fanfare in 1939. In Canada, this prompted conjecture about hockey's mythical puck hall of fame and who would be eligible for such honours. Montreal's Ferguson kicked off the discussion in a 1940 Toronto Maple Leafs Garden program. "Nothing lends so much exultation to ancient performance as old Pa Time himself," he sneered. "He spreads fertilizer that surrounds the old timers in a haze of distant light, glorifies them into beings of super human endurance, skill and ability. Old tales of athletic splendour…gain in the telling, like a snowball rolling down the mountain. They become magnified over the years." Ferguson would go on to be honoured in the writers' section of the Hockey Hall of Fame and to contribute flowery citations for the pioneer stars.

"The Shores, Horners, Johnsons, Smiths, Goodfellows, Morenzes, Joliats, Hainsworths, Jacksons, Clancys, Conachers, Primeaus, Stewarts, Gottseligs, Auries, Trotters, the Cooks, Bill and Bun, the Bouchers, Murdochs, Sieberts—all these and more," he gushed. "They're marched and are marching into the mythical Hall of Fame, even though we won't recognize it until Time drapes a halo around their glamorous feats until they've acquired the aura of antiquity." All but a few of these 1930 stars made it to the Hall.

3. THE SUTHERLAND CUP

"The grand old sports general" carried on his duties as a past president of the OHA and CAHA, attending annual meetings and taking the occasional bow for his devoted contribution to the game. In November 1940, Sutherland received a well-deserved compliment. The OHA named the provincial Junior B championship trophy "The Sutherland Cup." His chief supporter at *The Whig-Standard*, William J. Walshe, commented: "Capt. Jim, like a prophet, is not generally appreciated in his own home town, but in all other parts of the Dominion, he is considered an outstanding authority on the game." Captain Sutherland was almost as famous as the players he celebrated. So high was the esteem for the Kingstonian that the OHA named the championship trophy for the new Junior B group, The Sutherland Cup. "Capt. James T. Sutherland just refuses to lose his interest in his beloved hockey," wrote Bunny Morganson of *The Toronto Telegram*. "He is back in the midst of hockey with his proposal to scrap bodychecking among junior and intermediate clubs." He also stuck to his guns on his birthplace beliefs.

"Capt. Jim, like a prophet, is not generally appreciated in his own home town, but in all other parts of the Dominion, he is considered an outstanding authority on the game."

The Kingston media heaped praises on the 69-year-old veteran. "His memory of games and incidents in the development of hockey is remarkable," said Walshe. "He can remember hockey happenings of his early days in the sport as well as this year's events." Sutherland's reminiscences, he added, would make one of the best books ever published on the great winter game. He wrote numerous pamphlets and papers on his favourite game but never a book.

On February 1, 1941, a bombshell was lobbed into

the birthplace debate. Montreal octogenarian John T. Knox walked into *The Gazette* office with bulky documents "carefully written in long hand and bound with clothespins." He repeated a claim he had made four years earlier that his father Michael Knox had played hockey in Montreal in 1837. Columnist Harold MacNamara gave his tale prominent space in a series of three articles detailing the names of players on three teams that participated and describing the sticks and puck—"five inches long, four inches wide and about an inch thick."

They called the game "ice hurling," the creative gentleman said—"because my father and the other Irish boys wanted to play 'hurling' Ireland's national game during the winter." However, he made the mistake of listing positions for the Dorchesters, Uptowns, and French-speaking Canadians using lacrosse terms such as "point" and "cover point and "home" that hadn't been in use in 1837. He even included "rover," which wasn't created for hockey until the 1890s. Despite being "bogus," this fanciful story was repeated for years after.

Captain Sutherland didn't blink. Two months later, at the Canadian Amateur Hockey Association's annual meeting in Calgary, the 71-year-old hockey zealot was appointed to a committee "to draw a history of the birth and development of hockey." Neither he nor CAHA officials made any mention of establishing a hall of fame or selecting a site. The captain, who led the way, told the press the committee, consisting of hockey's notable leaders—George Slater of Montreal and W.A. (Bill) Hewitt of Toronto—intended to write "a background for our national game. … It would be something of a broad nature," he promised, and "not specially to cover any certain village or town."

The news was greeted with positive reports by the Montreal writers who noted that "Canada's national game" should follow the hall of fame movement by golf and baseball. "Surely somewhere somehow, records can be found to prove how and when the game was started," commented *The Gazette* in 1941. "That's the task facing (the committee). It's a tough one but they can do it. Hockey needs its Hall of Fame because that is the only way the hardy pioneers of hockey can be given the honour that is their due. Without a Hall…the feats of the oldsters…and the rest will soon be forgotten."

The Montreal Star seconded the motion but left no doubt as to where such a shrine should be located. "If such a memorial is to be put on such an enduring foundation, it should be built and maintained in Montreal," declared O'Meara, who noted demands would be made by Kingston, Ottawa, or Montreal and added the famous last words: "Toronto isn't considered for a number of reasons." Oh, yes!

Guess which Ontario city grabbed the soap box! "Historic Kingston would be an ideal location for the shrine of the puck sport," chimed in *The Whig-Standard*. "The Hall of Fame would be lost in a large metropolis like Montreal." The Toronto *Star's* Andy Lytle boosted the idea of a Kingston bid. "Kingston seems to have the best claims—a direct drive should be made for the memorial. Capt. James Sutherland is carrying on an almost one-man crusade for the honour."

"Historic Kingston would be an ideal location for the shrine of the puck sport," chimed in **The Whig-Standard.** *"The Hall of Fame would be lost in a large metropolis like Montreal."*

The dance over where hockey started continued in the press. One wise McGill official even surmised: "It may be a fact that hockey developed gradually in more than one more than one centre." Capt. Sutherland had already conceded that Halifax might share the honour with Kingston through military connections, but he continued to support his storied hometown.

Years later, *The Champions' Book of Sports* reviewed how Kingston, "jealous of the distinctions claimed by its rival (Montreal), set up its own group of experts" and proved where the game started, but opined: "Most impartial historians regard these claims as rather flimsy." Sutherland supporters held their ice. *Globe and Mail* columnist Ralph Allen stated confidently: "Cap'n Jim…is till unbeaten, untied and unscored on after more than 50 years amiable plugging of Kingston as the birthplace of hockey."

Some Montrealers would not accept that unblemished record, and one ex-patriot living in Los Angeles, California told sports historian Menke: "I originated the game of ice hockey on November 10, 1879." That was W.L. (Chick) Murray, who first unveiled the story six years earlier in *The McGill University Gazette*. The former student claimed he wrote the rules in concert with classmate W.F. Robertson, who had seen field hockey played in England, ordered sticks from a sample he had brought home. It had caused quite a controversy and some people did not accept his story—including Sutherland.

Throughout 1941 and into 1942, the dedicated Kingstonian was putting his years of experience to good use and his version of hockey's origin on paper.

He had little input from the other two committee members, who had decades of involvement in the game in Toronto and Montreal. Hewitt applauded him for doing a good job. "I have just read your very interesting report…and think it should not be altered one iota," the Toronto hockey mogul wrote to Sutherland late in March 1942. "Let the facts as you have collected them, speak for themselves." In a footnote he promised to observe "strict confidence" in the matter.

A month later, April 17, 1942, Sutherland presented a four-page printed report under the title, "The Origin of Hockey in Canada," set in old English type. He mentioned Montreal and Halifax but clearly defined Kingston as the genesis of the sport. There was no doubt that the paper was a "Sutherland report." Montreal's George Slater declined to take any credit. "I have not done a streak of work on this." However, he did advise his CAHA colleagues that he had some "recently gathered information," that he would like to submit. It was too little—too late.

The backlash against the findings of "the venerable Trinity" was led by Montreal oracle O'Meara. While granting that Sutherland "had scored again," Montrealers could prove "beyond all manner of doubt that the game had its first intelligent presentation in Montreal." Days later, he kept the pot boiling in his "Passing Sport Show" column by maintaining that Halifax had something to do with "the early origin of the game."

Should we not all admit that the origin of hockey is still obscure and cease making statements which have no foundation in fact.

On May 6, 1942, while staying in Montreal's Windsor Hotel, Sutherland dispatched a copy of the Origins report with a note indicating it had been revised "as suggested during visit to my room," and commented: "I think the revision rounds out the report about as well as we can hope for." The minor changes had no affect on F.M. Van Wagner, an assistant physical director at McGill University who had been monitoring the game's history as compiled by colleagues over the previous decade. On the same date, he submitted a strong statement to *The Montreal Star* that must have caught Sutherland's attention: "We have reached the unfortunate stage where many individuals are much more concerned with producing evidence and convincing the public that a certain individual originated the game, or that a certain city was its birthplace, than they are in learning the truth about the origin of hockey."

Van Wagner zeroed in on Sutherland's claim that was based on a Kingston historian's diary of shinny being played there in the mid-1840s. "Let us not confuse the origin of (field) hockey or hurley with that of hockey, or I am afraid we will be led far back in history for the Greeks had a game played with crooked stick and a ball as early as the fifth century B.C. …the development from shinny to hockey was most natural and logical and for that reason it may be found impossible to trace the origin of hockey to a particular time and place." He concluded his letter to the *Star* with these profound words that ring true today: "Should we not all admit that the origin of hockey is still obscure and cease making statements which have no foundation in fact, while at the same time producing all the substantiated data possible that may contribute to our further knowledge of the early development of ice hockey."

Two weeks later, Van Wagner sent seven pages of typewritten single space text showing the history of the debate and repeating his plea for accuracy. Noting the many "mis-statements" and without naming Sutherland, he charged that the debaters tried to prove their claims by "reiteration rather than by presentation of sound evidence." In scholarly fashion, he submitted detailed descriptions of the game as a "recognized game" at McGill. He listed the names of players, descriptions of play and the "off-side" rule, against a Montreal team in 1877. Another keynote citation was reported on January 18, 1879, when *The McGill University Gazette* reported the size of the playing surface—50 yards long and 20 wide—and declared hockey had been played in Montreal "for more than three years."

He expressed dismay as to why Halifax had never been given serious consideration as the birthplace of hockey and pointed out the references to the Halifax rules. "Our attempts to have some Halifax residents look into the matter some years ago proved unsuccessful. Some historian," he added, "will have to be trusted with responsibility of weighing all evidence and making an unbiased decision."

In reply to Van Wagner, Sutherland trotted out his own anecdotal evidence. In his "younger days" he recalled chatting with ex-members of the Royal Canadian Rifles…who settled in Kingston after the regiment disbanded in 1869-70. "Many of these men (who joined banks, customs, and the police force), had their tales to tell about the grand game they had played in the Old Land and in the RCR (in Kingston).

Frank Menke, the American sports historian, dispatched the Sutherland report as "a document devoid of established facts."

Sutherland threw Van Wagner one bone: "I think that you are to be congratulated for the effort you have made in the matter," he wrote "and trust that you will realize that you have at least been a contributing factor in the whole matter." To which the Montrealer appended a hand written note to a colleague: "This evades the issue and still leaves the report of his committee as accurate and final." The Montreal-Kingston debate was just heating up! Frank Menke, the American sports historian, dispatched the Sutherland report as "a document devoid of established facts."

Bobby Hewitson, esteemed Toronto newspaperman and future Hockey Hall of Fame curator, summed up the situation this way: "Out of all the claims and counter-claims of the cities seeking to have the honour of originating the winter pastime, Kingston and Montreal represented the strongest front, while Halifax did not offer too strong a presentation." However, Haligonian "guns" would not remain silent for long.

The Passing Sport Show

By "Baz" O'Meara

The Montreal Daily Star, Wednesday, Jan. 3, 1934

THERE will be less murmuring in the market places today in those spots where Maroons supporters meet to moan over the good old days of the Big S line. As the boys grow garrulous over their enhanced memories they may do a bit of peering into the future, out of which may emerge a vision, dream or possibly a mirage depicting Maroons in rousing final playoffs by

* * *

"**O**LD Man Hockey" was talking about scoring feats when the discussion drifted back to the old timers. "I remember once when Frontenac's beat Belleville 33-3 in one game then 10-0 in another," he reminisced. "Scotty Davidson must have scored sixteen goals in that game. We didn't keep accurate records, but I remember we figured he had jammed in half those scores." "Old man Hockey" is Jim Sutherland than whom there is no greater storehouse of hockey information in the country. Out of Kingston as often as he can be, he has that intense loyalty to the old

Although he strongly disagreed with Captain Sutherland on the birthplace of hockey, Montreal's leading sports columnist, Baz O'Meara, saluted the 64-year-old as "Old Man Hockey" and lauded his "storehouse" of information. He was one of several sports writers who battled over the birthplace question for two decades.

SPORTDOM
by "Gee" Ahern

FAITH finally triumphed for Pictou Royals in their series with ... season as unbeatable in the Mari-

Assorted Sports
By Wm. J. Walshe
SPORTS EDITOR

Kingston is now competing with all Canada in the flood of claims for the hockey hall of fame and a powerful committee, well supported by facts and finances, will be needed to convince the controlling powers that the shinny shrine should be located in the city where the sport was organized and first played. Charles Edwards, who writes the Canadian Press "Sports Snapshots," refers to the recent rush of applications as a Dominion-wide sweepstakes, with the move that started in Halifax going almost completely across the continent.

Stratford's sports editor, Chick Appel, of the Beacon Herald, is a trifle off the beacon in his suggestion that Ottawa should have the hall of fame as the scene of the first organized hockey in 1889. Royal Military College and Queen's played a schedule of games four years

The Nova Scotian case was strengthened by the concerted efforts of another authority, J.E. (Gee) Ahearn, a Halifax alderman and sportsman. He opened the debate as to what players should qualify for hall of fame honours.

William J. (Bill) Walshe, sports editor of The Whig-Standard, was Sutherland's right-hand man in promoting the city as the birthplace of hockey in his daily column, Assorted Sports.

Frank G. Menke

Distinguished Americans sports historian Frank G. Menke (left) supported Kingston's claim at first, but came around to backing Montreal and Halifax as birthplaces. He authored the 1930 All-Sports Record Book *and the* Encyclopedia of Sports. *He made a fervent plea to Capt. Sutherland for facts, not opinions, and called for "needed delicacy" with Montreal claimants.*

F.M. Van Wagner

Floyd Marcellus Van Wagner, who answered to "Van," was an American trained phys-ed instructor and a McGill basketball coach, who skillfully defended the university's hockey claims. He penned a scholarly paper, "Origin and Development of Ice Hockey," which the CAHA and NHL unwisely ignored.

The Ontario Hockey Association honoured Capt. Sutherland when they named the OHA Junior B championship trophy in his name in 1940. It is now awarded to the Greater Ontario Junior Hockey League champions.

𝔒𝔯𝔦𝔤𝔦𝔫 𝔬𝔣 𝔥𝔬𝔠𝔨𝔢𝔶 𝔦𝔫 𝔠𝔞𝔫𝔞𝔡𝔞

REPORT

submitted to the

Canadian Amateur Hockey Association

Annual Meeting - Royal York Hotel

•

Toronto, Ontario

April, 1942

Montreal Gazette "Solely"

WEDNESDAY, OCTOBER 6, 1943.

Sutherland Defends Claims Of Kingston to Hall of Fame

According to a letter received by Athletic Commission Chairman Frank Hogan from Captain James Sutherland of the Kingston "Hall of Fame" committee, the Kingstonians' demand that their city be awarded the "Hall" plum was never based on their assumption that Kingston saw Canada's first game of hockey. Sutherland claims that their chief reason for defending their city as the logical "Hall" site was because of its very central position, almost exactly halfway between Toronto and Montreal.

While this may be reason enough for Kingston getting the award, from their point of view at least, it still leaves the true site of Canada's first game of hockey very much up in the air and can hardly be considered a direct answer to the Montreal Commission's polite request for the support of the Kingston body in stimulating some semblance of a National round-table, the only just and permanent method of discovering the true site of the nation's first hockey game.

The Commission's similar letters of request to Frank Sargeant, C.A.H.A. head, and Mervyn "Red" Dutton, N.H.L. leader, are unanswered as yet. Until all the interested bodies have shown their hands, little more can be done about a movement that the late Frank Calder, long-time N.H.L. head, stoutly insisted should be treated strictly as a post-war project, advice which the Montreal Commission has followed to the letter, the chief reason for their being one of the last to enter the discussion.

A three-man committee appointed by the Canadian Amateur Hockey Association released the Origin of Hockey in Canada *report in April 1942. Written by Capt. Sutherland, it strongly favoured Kingston as the game's birthplace and the best home for a hockey hall of fame.*

In his response to criticism of the Kingston claim, Sutherland clipped The Montreal Gazette *story and inserted the word "solely" to clarify the basis for the Kingston argument.*

The "All-Time All-Stars" of Hockey 1900—1939

By W. A. HEWITT

W.A. (Billy) Hewitt, a noted hockey administrator for 40 years, led off the debate as to what players should be elected to the Hall of Fame. Current stars and pioneer players were nominated to the "Paper" hall.

"It's too bad that hockey can't show us its birth certificate. It would save a lot of digging and delving. It has had a lot of relations— shinny, houquet, hurley—and right now the question is up again as a trio of Canadian cities are claiming the popular old sport as their very own." — Frank Power, Halifax Herald, March 2, 1943

THE WAR OF 1943

1. BATTLE FOR THE HALL

Hockey in its 135-year history has recorded some landmark years—none more notable than 1893 when Lord Stanley donated the Dominion Hockey Trophy for the championship of Canada (now called the Stanley Cup). Five decades later there was another cardinal point in the game's history. In 1943, moguls of the ice sport—from the CAHA to the NHL—got serious about its history. They delved into its origin and decided after heated debate to create a home for hockey—a hall of fame—to honour its greats and provide an archive for its storied past. For 40 years, it was a toss-up between the Ontario city of Kingston and the Quebec metropolis of Montreal as to where the game originated. In 1943, the pendulum swung to the east coast city of Halifax.

In the *Halifax Herald*, columnist Ken Chisholm swung the debate from "Birthplace" to "Hall of Fame" by reporting the City of Halifax's action: "City Council has already given approval to the idea of establishing such a hall of fame in this city which has been associated with the great ice game since 1860." The mayor planned to appoint three aldermen and three citizens to "get after the NHL" and seek their blessing. The Kingston columnist Walshe pointed out that Sutherland for years had almost been the lone voice crying in the wilderness to attract attention to Kingston's claim. "He had pamphlets printed years ago to establish Kingston's right to the honour, but until Halifax made a claim, he had not received any support … He knows every person who would have a vote in declaring the scene of the shrine."

Chisholm predicted a successful bid would bring proper recognition all over the United States and Canada to the national game and to players "whose names will live forever in hockey wherever the Hall is setup." He, along with fellow sports writer W.J. (Ace) Foley and Alderman J.E. (Gee) Ahearn, were appointed by Mayor W.E. Donovan to a six-man committee to investigate and promote a hall of fame bid. *The Herald* sounded optimistic trumpets for the project: "Local historians claim Halifax has the number one claim as the birthplace of hockey and scoff at any attempt to share the honour with Montreal or Kingston." Both cities had made unofficial gestures but Halifax's bid was acknowledged by the NHL's interim president Red Dutton. The former New York American player and coach had succeeded the late Frank Calder, who had urged any "birthplace" discussions be deferred until after the war.

Chisholm, in his "Sports Slant" column, added another challenge to any city that might challenge Halifax's claim. "It might be a good idea—to settle the matter—for claimants to the 'first-game' title to produce the records of their early encounters." No one accepted the challenge.

Veteran Toronto sportsman Charlie Querrie jumped into the fray in November 1943 and produced the first serious summary of the project, complete with nominations for referees, "net guardians, defence men of class, centre men of fame" and prominent wingers. A regular contributor to the Toronto Maple Leaf Gardens' program, he noted that hockey's first shrine would be located in Kingston and commented: "This has already started Halifax on the warpath, but the site will probably remain in Kingston, unless Halifax can find someone who can out-talk or out-argue one James Sutherland of Kingston."

In Halifax, Gee Ahearn, a former amateur and pro

player in the Maritimes and Eastern United States, suggested possible honourees for Canada's first hockey shrine: Cyclone Taylor, Hod Stuart, Hamby Shore, Newsy Lalonde, Howie Morenz, Frank Nighbor, Tom Phillips, Sprague Cleghorn, Russell Bowie, and Hobey Baker. All but Hamby Shore were eventually elected to the shrine.

The site will probably remain in Kingston, unless Halifax can find someone who can out-talk or out-argue one James Sutherland of Kingston.

The list set-off a guessing game that pundits and fans play every season. The aggressiveness of the east coasters took Kingston by surprise. "Kingston should move fast if it wants the proposed hockey Hall of Fame as a tourist attraction," responded the *Whig-Standard*'s W.J. (Bill) Walshe. The Limestone City, backed by the Chamber of Commerce, decided to make an official claim. "If Capt. Sutherland is put in charge of a Kingston committee to bid for the Hall of Fame, Kingston's chance of success would be greater," Walshe added. "He has enough statistics to support his claim and experience in the inner sanctum of hockey governments."

2. TORONTO ENTERS THE FRAY

Out of Toronto came an odd comment that over the years would prove quite prophetic. Andy Lytle of *The Toronto Star* quoted Manager Frank Selke of the Toronto Maple Leafs as saying Toronto would be willing to house a hall of fame. "The basis for Toronto's claim is not clear," said Lytle, "unless it is the fact that Maple Leaf Gardens has a couple of spare rooms available for the purpose."

Lytle wondered out loud, "Who cares about where hockey originated?" and the reply resounded from Halifax's Frank Power. "Kingston, Montreal and Halifax do care. They care a whole lot!" The Halifax press was peppered with reminiscences of the Mic Mac Indians producing sticks and playing the game on the Northwest Arm and the Dartmouth lakes. "The origin of hockey has been talked about and argued over for many years," commented *The Herald*. "A half dozen years ago it was figuring prominently in the sports news and discussion became hot." It was due to heat up. The NHL announced in March 1943 that it would consider bids in May of that year. Kingston would be the challenger to match Halifax's early bid.

Early in April 1943 the Kingston Hall of Fame Committee asked for recognition of Kingston as the birthplace of hockey, and City Council offered the

Canadian Amateur Hockey Association space in City Hall "which overlooks the bay where the first game of hockey was played." CAHA President Frank Sargent noted that the subject of a Hall had never been discussed at an association meeting and placed the Kingston request on the agenda for the upcoming annual meeting in Port Arthur, Ontario (now Thunder Bay). Sutherland held the floor and painted an optimistic picture of the project, matching baseball's hall of fame with a tablet reading: "This Hall of Fame has been dedicated to perpetuate the memory of the men who have done so much to develop nationally and internationally Canada's great winter sport." It would, he promised, recognize all provincial hockey organizations, at no cost to them. "Personally, I think it would be regrettable should this association postpone favourable action."

City Council offered the Canadian Amateur Hockey Association space in City Hall "which overlooks the bay where the first game of hockey was played."

"There's a war on—What's the hurry?" countered W.A. Fry of Dunnville, Ontario. "If you defer action," Sutherland replied, "The heat is off."

"I think it would be a splendid thing to have such a building in Canada and I think it should be as central as possible," Sutherland told his colleagues. "This is not a Kingston Hall of Fame; it is your Hall of Fame, Canada's Hall of Fame, a national affair." The placing of it in Kingston, he added, would be a recognition of Kingston's long service in organized hockey. "Kingston being located half-way between Toronto and Montreal is ideal!"

The CAHA delegates stuck to their guns, and despite Kingston's reported invitation to attend the NHL meetings on May 7-8, accepted the resolutions' committee ruling that the matter of a site for the proposed Hall be left to officers in conjunction with those in hockey's professional organizations.

On Sutherland's return to his hometown, William Walshe predicted "Kingston would not get the Hall of Fame without a fight and in fighting will have to be prepared for rough and tumble exchanges," citing a report from Halifax. *The Whig-Standard* scribe, in retrospect, was spot on. "We've got the goods to convince the NHL that Halifax is the proper place to establish a hall of fame," Gee Ahearn, secretary of the Halifax committee. "Evidence will be placed before league officials at their next meeting. The committee is convinced the first game of hockey ever played in Canada took place in this old garrison city at least 25 years before Kingston."

Kingston would not get the Hall of Fame without a fight and in fighting will have to be prepared for rough and tumble exchanges.

Some of "the goods"—including opposition to Kingston—came from Halifax historian John W. Regan, author of *First Things in Acadia,* published in 1936. "It is a fact…that for years—1860 to 1890 and after —thousands of pairs of skates and hundreds of bundles of Indian-made hockey sticks were regularly shipped from Dartmouth, Halifax and Saint John to sporting goods houses in New England, Montreal, and Toronto for local distribution…Hockey or hurley did not start in the Maritimes at Confederation (1867) but long before."

Scholar Regan, in exchanges with McGill University officials, delved into the crude implements used in the early games and queried the meaning of the word "puck" and the source of "Halifax Rules." McGill athletic manager Hay Finlay sent him a sketch of the blade of a hockey stick in the McGill "archives" purportedly used between 1878 and 1881. "The hockey diagram is an exact picture of the Indian sticks of former days," he replied. "The whole tree was sacrificed by the Indians, to get the roots which authorities objected to and the supply of bent shapes was exhausted after a number of years, especially following growing demand."

McGill's Van Wagner continued the dialogue with Halifax officials and made one point clear: "While we do not claim to possess sufficient evidence to prove that hockey originated in Montreal or at McGill, there does seem to be sufficient evidence to show beyond a doubt that if it was not actually born here, at least this is where it was nurtured and grew up." He was adamant on another key point. "Any statement regarding the origin of hockey which fails to distinguish between hockey and shinny throws no light on the origin of hockey." Montreal officials heated up their "birthplace" offensive as the summer of 1943 warmed up. So did the rhetoric—some of it positive and helpful. "Each bit of new evidence that comes to light brings us just that much nearer the day when the story of the origin of hockey can be written," said McGill Physical Education director Van Wagner in a June 24th letter to Halifax author John Regan. "In our search for the origin of hockey, facts are what we seek. Opinions we all have, but when stated publicly they often only confuse the issue," Van Wagner noted in another letter to Regan, dated November 24, 1943.

A discerning light was about to focus on the argument from the south.

3. KINGSTON CONQUERS

In 1943, William J. Walshe at *The Whig-Standard* noted that "the once dead debate has been revived by Frank G. Menke…who is dragging into the open again the skeleton of an argument as to the origin of hockey, its place of birth and with it the location of the Hall of Hockey Fame." The old but familiar voice of sports historian Frank Menke spoke up from New York. "There has been so much dispute as to who originated hockey, when and where, that I want to run it down to a definite point," he told McGill's long-time athletics director A.S. Lamb. He accepted most of Dick Smith's statement about the beginnings at McGill as supported by classmates Frederic Hague, but found Chick Murray's version "illogical." He thought it was odd that Murray has Robertson, a senior, appealing to him, a freshman, for mental guidance in devising a new game. "I am not very familiar with college etiquette in Canada, but in the States a senior usually regards a freshman as something that should be seen and never heard, and not seen too often."

With the tact of a district attorney, newsman Menke wrote Captain Sutherland and challenged his Origins report. "I have asked him for FACTS, asked him to name the papers, or records, or give me quotes from authentic letters. He has brought the challenge upon himself. He made a search for the origin of the game, and presented conclusions as facts designed, perhaps unintentionally, to brush aside the Smith and McGill claim."

Regan was definitely on Orlick's side of the debate—favouring facts over opinions. "We cannot conscientiously piously profess no interest in the birthplace of hockey, but certainly adhere strictly to the postulate that the facts must govern…Owing to so many phony claims…which once for all require to be nipped in the bud, before the disease becomes epidemic." On June 5, 1943, Regan added, "Hockey on the ice had been second nature with Maritimers, records show, long before the game became common in Centralist communities (Ontario and Quebec.).

Menke, amidst conflicting reports out of Montreal and Kingston in July 1943, admitted he was perplexed. "Sutherland wrote me only a week ago, and still is vehement about Kingston," he wrote Lamb. "If I ignore them, they will think it was done to shut them out; if I reprint their stories, they might not like to see what's in print. Also, if I don't print the Smith, Murray, and Sutherland versions, the intriguing part of the history of this modern game is lost. Within the lifetime of the oldest inhabitants, hockey was originated, developed, and made into a major game and yet there is not any indisputable data."

The debate switched from a whimper to a bang on September 10, 1943, when the NHL endorsed a proposal to establish at the Hall of Fame at Kingston.

While working on the hockey chapter in the next edition of *The Encyclopedia of Sports*, Menke offered to send a proof copy to Van Wagner for an opinion "on whether the matter was handled with the needed delicacy."

Meanwhile, Halifax's John Regan continued his dialogue with Montreal officials, critiqued Kingston claims, and accepted "hurley and hockey" as similar games but not "shinny." While admitting Halifax had difficulty finding "a competent and reliable person" to do the reviewing, he declared the proceedings would not touch shinny, bandy "or other fugitive ice sport."

The debate switched from a whimper to a bang on September 10, 1943, when the NHL endorsed a proposal to establish the Hall of Fame at Kingston. Key to the acceptance, besides Capt. Sutherland's strong and sustained leadership, was the appearance before the governors of Bill Cook, the great New York Ranger star, whose old boss Lester Patrick said Kingston was the obvious place being situated halfway between Toronto and Montreal. Cook, then coaching the AHL Cleveland Barons, was strongly supported by Kingston Alderman Ed Charlton. The former Montreal resident and world traveller, well briefed by Sutherland, spent days in the Quebec metropolis currying support for the Limestone City. The authorities, said Kingston's Walshe, succumbed practically "under the persuasive eloquence of Jim Sutherland."

The NHL decision delighted Kingstonians, none more than the man who led the initiative. "We had to fight for it, but we won recognition," an exuberant Sutherland told the local press. Ten days later the CAHA officers endorsed the NHL ruling and reported the shrine would be housed in Kingston City Hall, as wartime restrictions prevented construction of a permanent Hockey Hall. When peace prevailed, it was expected that the museum would become part of a proposed new civic arena. This round of events proved once again that, in the words of William J. Walshe, Sports Editor at *The Whig-Standard*, that "Captain Sutherland is a soldier and a sportsman by heritage."

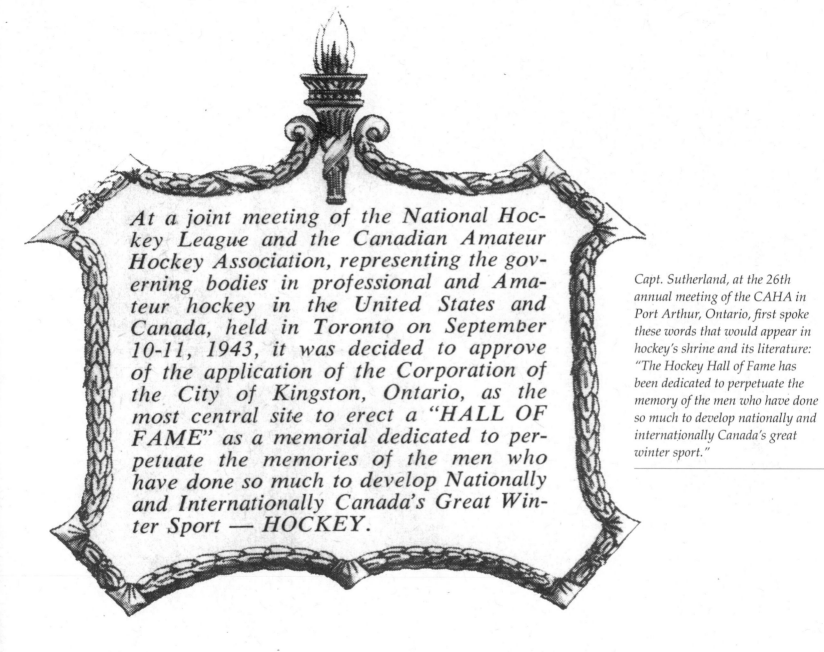

At a joint meeting of the National Hockey League and the Canadian Amateur Hockey Association, representing the governing bodies in professional and Amateur hockey in the United States and Canada, held in Toronto on September 10-11, 1943, it was decided to approve of the application of the Corporation of the City of Kingston, Ontario, as the most central site to erect a "HALL OF FAME" as a memorial dedicated to perpetuate the memories of the men who have done so much to develop Nationally and Internationally Canada's Great Winter Sport — HOCKEY.

Capt. Sutherland, at the 26th annual meeting of the CAHA in Port Arthur, Ontario, first spoke these words that would appear in hockey's shrine and its literature: "The Hockey Hall of Fame has been dedicated to perpetuate the memory of the men who have done so much to develop nationally and internationally Canada's great winter sport."

The International Hockey Hall of Fame

as designed by architects for approval, is shown above. Built of stone, matching Kingston's main buildings, the hockey memorial should blend into the scheme of Kingston's limestone tradition. The site for the shrine has not been selected but if ambitions are realized it will be on property in the down-town section. About 50 feet wide, with two floors—the lower floor to be known as "The Hall of Honor," the upper floor "The Museum" for hockey relics and souvenirs—the building should prove an attractive addition to Kingston's many beautiful buildings and a suitable shrine for Canada's great winter game. The estimated cost is expected to be around $50,000.

Hall of Fame directors moved quickly to plan the building. When the Baseball Hall of Fame opened in Cooperstown, New York, in 1939, Capt. Sutherland had seized the opportunity to inspect the shrine, and Kingston architects were now asked to create some of the building's features in an artist's conception of a hockey hall of fame.

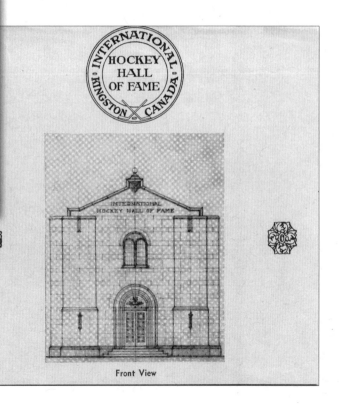

Front View

The Memorial Centre grounds became the preferred location of the Hall of Fame after several downtown locations were rejected.

BUILDING A SHRINE

(1945-1949)

1. CONSTITUTIONAL AFFAIRS

In time, "the shrine would pay for itself," a *Whig-Standard* writer predicted. The Ontario city would also cash in on the tourist traffic and world-wide advertising. "Like Cooperstown in baseball, Kingston would be known as the home of hockey wherever the game is played." Not quite! In contrast, *Toronto Star* columnist Andy Lytle summed up the decision this way: "I guess the NHL…was finally glad enough to let Jim Sutherland and his cohorts have it on the assumption that it was a headache anyway you looked at it and would never play to sell out crowds anyway."

Fourteen days after Kingston received the go-ahead, prominent citizens and sportsmen attend Council to hear Capt. Sutherland review the project and to make preliminary plans to promote the Hall.

Alderman Stuart Crawford was elected president and a full slate of 35 officers was named to various committees, with Captain Sutherland serving as an honorary member of all committees. The honorary presidents included premiers, senators, generals, colonels, aldermen, and former pro hockey players still active in the game—W.O. (Bill) Cook, F.J. (Bun) Cook, and W.D (Wally) Elmer.

The honorary presidents included premiers, senators, generals, colonels, aldermen, and former pro hockey players still active in the game—W.O. (Bill) Cook, F.J. (Bun) Cook, and W.D (Wally) Elmer.

On Sutherland's suggestion, a board of governors was named. Given the honour of selecting Hall members for the first Hall of Fame were Lester (Silver Fox) Patrick of the New York Rangers, Red Dutton, President of the NHL, representatives of the CAHA and OHA, and two leading newspapermen in Toronto and Montreal, plus sportsman Abbie Cook of Winnipeg.

Oblivious to public perception, Sutherland and Company moved ahead at another general meeting on February 12, 1944. The Kingston committee approved a constitution, some of which was based on the bylaws of the Baseball Hall of Fame.

Article 3A stipulated the objects of the hockey heritage organization:

> "To establish, build and perpetuate… an international memorial for the game of ice hockey, its players and officials (both professional and amateur) who have distinguished themselves with the game of ice hockey since its beginning to the present time and in perpetuity."

Subsequent clauses laid out the goals to build and maintain a shrine where the history of the game would be recorded, and where replicas and souvenirs of the game may be received and exhibited "and appropriate memorials and testimonials of selected members displayed."

One would think the NHL-CAHA decisions to award Kingston the palm would put an end to the great debate over where the game started. Instead, it intensified. The joint decision irked the Haligonians. Reeking of sarcasm, the *Halifax Herald*'s Chisholm retorted: "Maritimers would have to have a replay of early games here with the original players taking part, before any claim from this section would get to first base." Kingston had only won the first round of this prize fight.

One would think the NHL-CAHA decisions to award Kingston the palm would put an end to the great debate over where the game started. Instead it, intensified.

The Halifax committee recruited Industry and Publicity Minister and one-time athlete Harold Connolly to press its case and launch a protest. He maintained the NHL acted hastily and based the decision on incomplete and inaccurate information. In making the announcement, *The Herald* said: "If decided not on merit but best tourist attraction, Montreal or Ottawa would be far more suitable than Kingston."

Kingston's Walshe rallied: "Most of the Montreal claims are legends, memories of old men, who are recalling conversations they had in the dim and distant past." He maintained such a hall would be lost in Montreal, Toronto, or Ottawa and "out of the way in Halifax." "In Kingston it will be one of the big historical attractions." He said the award was made to Kingston, not only because it had a good birthplace claim, but most on its central location for visitors.

"The idea of the Hall is to perpetuate the memory of great stars and leaders of the game, not to honour any special place as the scene of the first game. Museums are established not where relics are found, but in places where they may be seen, studied or respected by the greatest numbers."

A new and learned voice entered the discussion in September when Baz O'Meara interviewed J. Clem Beauchamp, an Ottawa civil servant who was convinced the Orlick/McGill claims were justified. The former newspaperman, who had contributed articles on hockey's history, was lauded by *The Montreal Star* sports editor: "He has a judicial mind and manner. He weighs evidence carefully. He has no interest in civicism or parochialism." Just what the debate needed, but was it too late?

The reaction in Montreal remained hostile. McGill's E.M. (Em) Orlick was flabbergasted at the NHL decision. In the first of a series of four articles in *The Gazette*, the man with the initials "M.S. Dip. M.S.P.E." behind his name, penned an Open Letter to NHL Governors. "I am convinced that those responsible for making the decision were victims of the greatest hoax perpetuated in the annals of Canadian sport," he blasted. "I am flabbergasted to say the least that Kingston has been selected. I am thoroughly conversant with the official

CAHA Report on the Origin of Ice Hockey but never dreamed that anyone could possibly give such an obviously prejudiced and historically incorrect conglomeration of dogmatic assertions a second thought."

In the third articles of the series, Orlick said many fingers from the past point toward Halifax as "the seat of ice hockey." Unfortunately, no irrefutable evidence was uncovered. He then set out a six-step program for the CAHA to follow in setting up a tribunal—three-man research committees in Montreal, Halifax and Kingston—comprising professional historians from universities in the three cities. "Let them know that dogmatic statements, unsubstantiated conclusions and hearsay evidence is definitely not wanted."

In his fourth and final article, he repeated verbatim press reports of the 1870s games and commented in scholarly fashion on their significance. "Though the evidence reproduced here represents only about one-tenth of that in my possession, I am sure that sufficient has been presented to convince even the most skeptical that all of my earlier statements can be backed by authentic facts." In closing, he pleaded for "fair-play and true sportsmanship," again appealed to the authorities to accept only "authentic documented evidence," and offered to present his findings to any committee of recognized historians—all to no avail.

Orlick continued his search for authenticity. He struck gold in November 1943 when he contacted a prominent Montreal businessman who had played in the first recorded game in the city in March 1875. In an interview published in *The Gazette*, 88-year-old Henry Joseph opened up a new leaf in Canadian hockey history. Backed by Orlick's research, the one-time player identified 14 of 17 men who played in the initial indoor game and credited Halifax native James George Aylwin Creighton with introducing the game—nine a side—with rules based on English rugby. "It was this exhibition," said Orlick, "which aroused city-wide interest and gave rise to the formation of other hockey teams in the city and to the rapid development of the game which my original series of articles outlined."

Ironically, the Montreal reaction to the Kingston award was in stark contrast to the citizen's action when the Hall of Fame movement was first proposed by sportsman Leo Dandurand in 1940. "Montreal just yawned," said O'Meara. "Yawning is not only an art in Montreal sports circles but a career."

"The question of re-opening the Hall of Fame affair may serve some academic but it won't get anywhere," predicted O'Meara. Sutherland stepped into the breach and maintained that Kingston's bid for the Hall was never based solely on the assumption that Kingston saw Canada's first game of hockey. The chief reason for defending their city as the logical Hall site was because of its central position, almost exactly halfway between Toronto and Montreal.

"The question of re-opening the Hall of Fame affair may serve some academic but it won't get anywhere."

In November, two months after Kingston got the nod, Halifax was still pressing its claim for the shrine. Historian Regan, who had claimed to be an independent observer in the debate, was granted $150 by Halifax City Council to prepare a brief on the East Coast city's claims. He was upstaged by Menke, who had credited Montreal as the birthplace of hockey, refuted the Kingston claim, and performed a switch by supporting Halifax.

"Hockey was first played in Halifax and the Hall should be in that city," he declared in an interview at his Fairfield, Connecticut home. "All I could find shows it was first played in Halifax by Scottish regiments and then adopted later by Montreal athletes. There's no coherent record of the game being played in Kingston before the mid 1880s."

From December 14 to 31, 1943, Menke published a 10-part series covering his findings in *The Halifax Herald* under the title "The Origin of Ice Hockey in Canada." *The Encyclopedia of Sports* author revived Nova Scotia hopes when he made this definitive statement in the final chapter: "It is my opinion that it originated in Halifax, was developed into the modern game in Montreal, then played in Ottawa and a short time later in Kingston."

In a Toronto Maple Leaf Gardens' program, Montreal's O'Meara could not resist one more observation: "So they settled the Hall of Fame in Kingston and everybody lived happily ever after." His research had provided most of the Menke material and he strove for the last word: "Kingston has the Hall of Fame, but will this Hall stand as a credit or a discredit to the city and for the sportsman responsible for having it erected there? Only time will tell and as it has been wisely said, 'Truth will out.'"

Four months after Kingston was awarded the Hockey Hall of Fame, opinions as to its proper city site were rampant and confusion continued to reign over the beginnings of the game. In Montreal, McGill officials were adamant that the NHL and CAHA had made a grave mistake. "There is only one city in the world where a Hockey Hall of Fame would justifiably be built—namely Montreal," Professor E.M. Orlick wrote in the winter edition of *The McGill News.* He urged the McGill Graduates' Society to make every effort to have the Kingston decision revoked and a new decision made in favour of Montreal.

Halifax rested its oars on Frank Menke's statement to historian Regan: "There does not seem to be any doubt that hockey first was played in Halifax." As to the site of the proposed shrine, other sources had varying opinions. "The Hockey Castle will be built in Kingston, unless Halifax can find someone who can out-talk and out-argue one James Sutherland," veteran Toronto sportsman Charlie Querrie commented in the Maple Leaf Gardens' program in 1943. "We doubt if anyone in Canada can out-do James when it comes to talking about the great hockey game."

The Kingston septuagenarian basked modestly in the applause and took a bow at a Toronto banquet where he was presented with a Gordon Medal as a life member of the OHA and CAHA. The presentation marked the Captain's diamond jubilee of 60 years associated with hockey. The *Whig-Standard*'s new sports editor, former *Globe* columnist Mike Rodden, praised "The Grand Old Man of Kingston Hockey" in pursuing the Hall of Fame project and gave a backhander to the citizens of the city he served: "The population of Kingston has never grasped the significance of this award." And they still do not grasp it.

He was presented with a Gordon Medal as a life member of the OHA and CAHA. The presentation marked the Captain's diamond jubilee of 60 years associated with hockey.

Despite this action in Kingston, McGill's Van Wagner continued his support of Montreal and his opposition to hockey's governing bodies. In a February 1944 article in Montreal's *Gazette,* under the title, "Origin and Development of Ice Hockey," he asked sarcastically: "Is there any evidence that the CAHA and the NHL are really interested in the origin of hockey?" The question fell on deaf ears.

The debate dipped into a discussion about the derivatives of hockey and the need for a hockey registrar. "There are, in reality, two games of hockey," said Van Wagner. "One is a game played by thousands of boys and young men throughout Canada. The other game is a highly organized business."

The NHL stuck to its business of making money while the perennial "birthplace" debate waxed and waned. Sutherland kept Kingston up front with thoughts about a suitable structure for the shrine that was hampered by wartime building restrictions. At a time when a good-sized home could be constructed for $5,000, he told the CAHA annual meeting at Montreal that "I am sure you would not be satisfied with an edifice at the cost of $15,000 or $20,000. So there is going to be something more imposing." He advised that a goal of $50,000 was set in order to build a two-storey building "with a curator's living quarters in the rear."

Hockey talk was pushed to the back pages as the invasion of Europe dominated the thoughts and minds of Canadians in June 1944. Five months later, with the days getting crisper, the words "Hockey" and "Birthplace" returned to the sports pages.

Sutherland took a different tack by publishing what the Canadian Press called "an instructive piece of literature on the origin of the game." In a four-page pamphlet, he related the history and rules of Bandy in England as told by the Eighth Duke of Beaufort but got in his two cents' worth on early history of Canadian hockey: "Here in Canada we have had several different opinions concerning the early history of ice hockey. It is well known that the writer has for many years claimed that the game in Canada was first played in Kingston and Halifax a century or more ago."

Supporters of the Montreal claim stuck with McGill's Orlick. *The Gazette*'s Dink Carroll, in his "Playing the Field" column, praised the professor for his research as "a labour of love" and predicted that the facts he unearthed would become part of the true, unwritten history of hockey. Much of Orlick's new data resulted in Frank Menke publishing a new edition of *The Encyclopedia of Sports* in 1944. Despite revelations from Montreal, he concluded that: "No one knows positively in what city, or what province, the game first was played…No one knows the year, or the approximate year, no one knows who pioneered it, what inspired it or who were the first players." And yet, he said, the available evidence pointed to Halifax.

He rightfully declared the history of the game has been confused by claims, counter-claims, erroneous information "and by men taking credit who never had earned credit for inventing ice hockey. They sensed an opportunity to gain some personal glory for devising the game, when there was little concern as to who devised it, and the efforts they made added to the confusion."

Halifax officials—led by newly-appointed Deputy Mayor Gee Ahearn—collected skates made in Dartmouth and kept the argument going with a bittersweet remark. "As all good Canadians know," he said, "ice hockey originated in Halifax many years before there was a Kingston." Sports editors still mused over why the Sutherland-led Kingston contingent won the day. Montreal's Carroll summed it up succinctly: "That innocuous-looking phrase, 'the most central site' covers one of the stiffest inner-city arguments to rage around the origin of hockey, since the game was invented." Sutherland agreed. "That seems to be the best way to get around it," he said. "No one can take offence at that."

Sports editors still mused over why the Sutherland-led Kingston contingent won the day.

The NHL seemingly closed the door on the site debate by approving "a substantial donation"—$7,500—to the building fund for the proposed shrine in Kingston. Thoughts then turned to choosing members to be in the homeless shrine. Article 4 of the newly written constitution stipulated "any person, living or dead is eligible to be duly selected to be honoured as a member of the International Hockey Hall of Fame." International, as indicated by the Union Jack and Stars and Stripes engravings on the constitution cover, meant residents or former residents of the Dominion of Canada or the United States of America. At that point in hockey's development with the NHL confined to six teams, no European was deemed worthy of consideration.

2. NINE IMMORTALS

Hockey history was made in the spring of 1945 when newly appointed governors of the selection committee were asked to fill out a simple but official ballot with instructions to "enter your most prominent choices in rotation" and to restrict their choices to 12. The eight nominees with the highest votes were to be selected. However, there was a tie for the last position. On May 1, nine former players were honoured posthumously. The inaugural inductees as memorialized in the International Hockey Hall of Fame's Roll of Honour Book were acknowledged by the leading sports writers of the day:

HOBART A. BAKER (1892-1918): *Blond, handsome, height 5' 9"—weight 160 pounds Hobey Baker, the greatest American-born player, by his easy, graceful skating, spectacular stick handling, exemplary sportsmanship and rare competitive ability.—Frank Ryan, Boston.*

CHARLES R. GARDNER (1904-1934): *Born in Scotland, Chuck Gardiner was one of hockey's great goaltenders when he died in St. Boniface hospital June 13, 1934, aged 30. He crammed considerable fame into life, won the Vezina Trophy twice and helped Chicago Black Hawks win the Stanley Cup.* —Abbie Coo. Winnipeg.

EDDIE GERRARD (1890-1937): *The amazing Ottawa athlete was one of the super-stars of hockey, football and paddling… He was a man who put as much energy into his performances that in his unswerving loyalty to his club he actually sacrificed his life. His keen sense of sportsmanship…commanded respect from all opponents.* —Mike Rodden, Kingston.

FRANK MCGEE (1881-1916): *The renowned centre of the Ottawa Silver Seven…had the use of only one eye. McGee was best remembered for his scoring feats …14 goals in one Stanley Cup game. He was an outstanding rugbyist … and a fine all-round sportsman.* —Basil O'Meara, Montreal.

HOWIE MORENZ (1902-1937): *Howie Morenz was a grand sportsman, who never engaged in a fight in his entire career — though he was a hard-driving, gallant and fearless players he was like a high strung thoroughbred, with a warm personality, a lovable boy with a million friends.* —Elmer W. Ferguson, Montreal.

TOM PHILLIPS (1883-1923): *This was the man who stole the thunder of the stars and became a national hockey figure almost over-night. A powerful and speedy skater, an adroit stickhandler, and the possessor of a wicket left hand shot, Phillips was one of the great stars of seven-man hockey.* —W.A. Hewitt, Toronto.

HARVEY PULFORD (1875-1940: *He was an outstanding defenceman with Ottawa for ten years…a fine football wingman, a great oarsman, paddler and squash player. The greatest all-rounder in the history of Canadian sport – a veritable titan on and off the playing fields.* —Basil O'Meara, Montreal.

HODGSON STUART (1879-1907): *Hod was one of the great defencemen of all time. He was Captain and Manager with Calumet in the International League, the first professional hockey league … and played for Montreal Wanderers when they won the Stanley Cup in 1906.* —George McNamara, Toronto.

GEORGES VEZINA (1887-1926): *He was one of the all-time hockey greats in the nets. He defied some of the greatest sharp-shooters of all time…standing there coolly and deflecting, or angling off the puck in a most uncanny way. He was truly a great goaler—and a figure of quiet dignity on or off the ice.*—Elmer W. Ferguson.

Captain Sutherland was honoured as a "Builder" of the sport along with pioneer administrators Frank Calder, John Ross Robertson, Francis Nelson, William A. Hewitt, William N. Northey, and Claude C. Robinson. "Through their combined efforts the game of hockey has developed its present thrilling hold upon all classes of people," said Sutherland. "Several of the 'Builders of Hockey' are still actively connected with the game, which goes to substantially prove that once one has swallowed the 'hockey germ' it remains with them during the whole period of their life."

The press release revealed that Morenz, Phillips, and Vezina led the way, while American amateur star Baker and Ottawa immortal Pulford were tied for eighth. One of the early supporters of Sutherland and the shrine was Michael James Rodden. "It was not an easy task that this veteran apostle of hockey so willingly shouldered," Mike wrote for Jim Hendy's NHL official *Hockey Guide* of 1946. "It could not be this way for there were others, long dormant, who hoped to grasp this Golden Fleece."

Rodden, in florid prose, wrote thumbnail sketches for the first nine Hall of Fame inductees—from "amazing defenceman" Hod Stuart—"who rated among the greatest them all"—to Montreal Canadiens' Howie Morenz—"probably the most colourful and publicized of all modern hockeyists." When the International Hockey Hall of Fame opened—ten years after Sutherland's death—Rodden tackled a tremendous task—"far more exacting than you would imagine," researching and writing the citations for 100 inducted members—each one hammered out on an Underwood typewriter and edited as only a veteran newsman would do.

An eternal guessing game—who should or shouldn't be in the hall of honour—had been launched in March 1943.

An eternal guessing game—who should or shouldn't be in the hall of honour—had been launched in March 1943 by Halifax sports writer Gee Ahearn.

He put forth 10 names, including Baker, Phillips, and Stuart, and seven others who eventually were elevated to the Hall. The names of the "first nine immortals" were entered in the Kingston shrine's Roll of Honour, together with a complete biography of each player. This beautiful book with black seal skin covering and ornate gold letters containing illuminated citations and a signed inscription from Governor General Alexander was proudly shown off by the creator of the Hockey Hall of Fame initiative.

"Capt. James T. Sutherland...is around town weighed down by a book which scales no less than 19 pounds," reported Montreal's Dink Carroll in May 1944. "The book, an impressive piece of workmanship, will some day be Exhibit A in the hockey museum. ... What will be in the shrine apart from this book containing the names of the game's immortals? he asked. "Well it seems there will be pictures of the men thus honoured."

There was little time for The Grand Old Man of Hockey to rest on his laurels. He and his Kingston mates and legal friends acquired a "Letters Patent" as a charitable organization to facilitate fundraising efforts for the project. This was completed before the third Hall of Fame game between the Toronto Maple Leafs and the Montreal Royals. And oddly enough the captain and crew had to continue defence of the title in what was called "the city of its birth."

3. RAISING FUNDS

The inaugural announcement of the "Original Nine" appeared to be a harbinger of peace as the six-year-long Second World War ended in August 1945 and Canadians turned to long postponed projects. Two proposals were launched in Kingston—one the construction of a modern arena and the other, the raising of funds for hospital expansion. Both took priority over any drive for the creation of a hockey shrine.

By 1946, the Kingston committee had $13,885.14 in cash and bonds in the bank and individuals and organizations were forwarding cheques large and small. Donations ranged from $5 from "a Brooklyn Supporter" to $5,000 granted by the Corporation of the City of Kingston and $10,000 awarded by the Canadian Amateur Hockey Association. In the first year of peace, 1946, Amateur Hockey Association of the United States sent a cheque for $1,100 and Canada's national organization, the Canadian Amateur Hockey Association topped all gifts with $10,000. Total raised: $32,740.14. Kingston citizens swelled the fund by

$4,225 with donations ranging from $25 to $500 contributed by Sutherland's shoe company—Scott & McHale Ltd.

The Kingston committee studying a suitable site for the shrine had been invited to locate it on the city's Fair Ground, which had been selected as the site of a new, postwar memorial arena.

In February 1946, a *Whig-Standard* headline heralded the news that Mayor Stuart Crawford had been re-elected president of the International Hockey Hall of Fame and that a generous donation ($1,000) had been made to the building fund by its chief supporter Sutherland, who sold his beloved launch to raise the amount.

The Kingston committee studying a suitable site for the shrine had been invited to locate it on the city's Fair Ground, which had been selected as the site of a new, postwar memorial arena. President Crawford opposed the site. "This being an international proposition, it should not be confused with our local undertakings, but should stand out alone," he declared. "The Hall of Fame we propose to build will be a distinguished substantial, fireproof building designed especially for the purpose of housing the collection reflecting the history and development of the international games and suitable plaques or pictures forming the gallery of the immortals within its walls." He got only half his wish.

Sutherland, despite devoting all his energy to the proposed hockey shrine, threw his support behind the fundraising drive for the community's memorial arena. In a letter to the editor, he noted Kingston's reputation as a city of considerable wealth and challenged the prospective donors. "Money is undoubtedly a very necessary thing…but there are some in our city who appear to be striving to be known as the richest person in Cataraqui (Cemetery)." The old soldier concluded his appeal with poetic words that applied to the proposed arena if not to the hockey shrine: "While poppies grow in a foreign land, in loyal Kingston, a fitting memorial must stand."

Rodden rallied for both causes but principally for the Hall of Fame, as he stated in a Kingston Saints' program: "It rightfully belongs to Kingston and will be erected here thanks to the vigilance and determination of one and only Jim Sutherland, the key man in this important enterprise." He predicted the Hall would become "a mecca for many Canadians and

Americans who visit Kingston at the gateway of the mighty St. Lawrence River each season." Captain Sutherland accepted the compliment and celebrated his 76th birthday by being elected president of the nine-team Kingston Hockey Association, an organization that dated back 56 years to the first city league in which he played.

James Sutherland and colleagues—despite postwar problems—kept up the good fight for the homeless Hall that lacked only money to bring it to life.

James Sutherland and colleagues—despite postwar problems—kept up the good fight for the homeless Hall that lacked only money to bring it to life. The mood wasn't all negative. In his 77th year, accolades and messages of appreciation and praise came his way. On January 27, 1947, James Thomas Sutherland and Clarence Sutherland Campbell, the new president of the National Hockey League, sat side-by-side in a rail seat at Kingston's Jock Harty Arena for an event that gave real impetus to the Hall's fundraising drive.

More than 2,600 hockey fans crammed into the arena operated by Queen's University to see Lester Patrick's New York Rangers meet the OHA Senior champion Hamilton Tigers. Led by two future Hall of Famers—Neil Colville and Edgar Laprade—the Broadway Blueshirts dominated Canada's leading amateurs, 5-2, in a free wheeling game in which silver-haired Mike Rodden, then 52, called only three minor penalties.

The Hall of Fame benefit game netted $3,593.58, a sum almost duplicated one month later when Boston Bruins scored a 5-3 victory over the same "Old Men of the Mountain" in the same Kingston rink. It was one of the last games ever played by Aubrey (Dit) Clapper, who two weeks earlier received his Hall of Fame certificate from President Crawford and Captain Sutherland at a pre-game ceremony in Boston Garden. After Bruins manager Art Ross and Frank (Pembroke Peach) Nighbor participated in the ceremonial face off, the 20-year veteran skated out in his old No. 5 jersey and took his defence position in front of Frank Brimsek, while fans were thrilled to see the soon-departed "Kraut Line" of Milt Schmidt, Bobby Bauer, and Porky Dumart, all RCAF veterans and future candidates for the Hall. Years later, Sutherland would proudly pose for pictures wearing Clapper's gold and black jersey.

February was a banner month for the burgeoning Kingston shrine. Sparked by Clapper's induction, the shrine formally welcomed its first group of seven living people, professionals and amateurs, by simple announcements in press and radio:

Professionals: Cyclone Taylor, Lester Patrick, Eddie Shore, Aurel Joliat, Frank Nighbor, Art Ross
Amateurs: Russell Bowie
Builders: Capt. James Sutherland

"These players...are moderns," Elmer Ferguson pointed out in *The Montreal Herald* in 1947. "That was a great era of hockey, of spectacular figures." Concerning the seventh inductee, Ferguson commented, "It's a wonder someone didn't think of Cap'n Jim before because he's the man responsible for the whole thing at Kingston, the man who for sheer love of the game has worked indefatigably to get the Hall established." The press release did not specifically credit Sutherland as "founder" of the Hall, but his official citation did in recognizing him for his "long and brilliant association with the game as a player and as hockey executive." As Ferguson concluded, "If anyone deserves a mythical niche in the Hall, it's this venerable enthusiast (Sutherland),"

Weeks later, "big, affable Jim Sutherland—a huge, white haired rumpled figure—blue eyes sparkling behind gold rimmed spectacles," was saluted in his hometown and in The Canadian Press as "one of the pillars on which Canadian amateur hockey has been built." The writer, managing editor of *The Whig-Standard* R.D. (Bob) Owen, said Sutherland had his heart set on two things: to raise sufficient money to finance the erection of the shrine and "to be on hand the day the doors first swing open."

Sutherland had his heart set on two things: to raise sufficient money to finance the erection of the shrine and "to be on hand the day the doors first swing open."

One of the shrine's early customs was to honour the enshrined in front of their fans, as was done with Clapper. It was repeated in Boston Garden for Eddie Shore, cited by Ferguson as "the burly, battling Bruin," the 'Mr. Hockey' of his day, the Bad Man of the League, and yet its most powerful figure." He was presented with a scroll by Hall President Crawford, and, in turn, presented his No. 2 sweater to Sutherland. Later that season Joliat was honoured during a game at the Montreal Forum.

John J. McHale of Scott & McHale of London,

Ontario, the shoe firm which Sutherland served for many of his 54 years as a salesman, added to the plaudits: "No man in Canada…has done more to further the interest of hockey in general and keep alive the spirit that makes it the great National Game of Canada—despite whatever claim might be made for Lacrosse— it is still Canada's National Game, and therefore I think it would be a very poor assembly of famous names in Hockey that did not include the name of Captain James T. Sutherland."

"THIS BUILDING WAS ERECTED HERE BECAUSE JIM SUTHERLAND KEPT THE FAITH!"

"The hall," said Mike Rodden, "is going to be erected here, and there in the largest letters should be: "THIS BUILDING WAS ERECTED HERE BECAUSE JIM SUTHERLAND KEPT THE FAITH!" The warm support came in response to another volley of criticism from American sports historian Frank Menke, who devoted most of seven hockey pages of the 1947 edition of the *New Encyclopedia of Sports* to review the age-old hockey debate. "No one in Canada of today or yesterday," he declared, "can say without contradiction when hockey was originated or where. It is unlikely the dispute will ever end." Menke dismissed the early Kingston shinny record, chided Halifax for not presenting factual evidence, and concluded: "On the basis of all the evidence so far unearthed, the answer to this question is that Ice Hockey started in the city of Montreal in 1875 and gradually evolved in Montreal into its present form."

Rodden, a Queen's University Arts graduate, stood behind Kingston's captain and responded with humor, citing a Biblical enforcer. "Jim Sutherland, having scanned the latest findings by Frank Menke and having perused the confused history of hockey as written in the McGill University hockey program, is firmly convinced that Menke and the McGill historians must be talking about some other game…when (Biblical strongman) Samson was knocking down those pillars by use of the body-check."

Sutherland wrapped up the momentous year of 1947 by joining Mayor Crawford in presenting a scroll to Lester Patrick, "testifying his admission to the Hockey Hall of Fame at Kingston, Ontario." The famous Ranger line of Bill and Bun Cook and Frank Boucher donned uniforms for the occasion "and did some passing stunts to remind the crowd of what used to be." Other dignitaries in the audience—Conny

Smythe, Frank Selke, Jack Adams, and NHL President Campbell—reported the *Star*'s Red Burnett, were greeted with "Bronx cheers." On a more positive note, the honored Mr. Patrick, introduced Capt. Sutherland at the Madison Square Garden dinner as "The Connie Mack of Hockey"—a complimentary tribute every American baseball fan could appreciate. Sutherland would have to squeeze home runs and dollars to provide a permanent home for distinguished inductees such as "The Silver Fox."

In the first week of the New Year, 1948, national and local hockey officials met at Kingston and witnessed an historic upset as Joe Primeau's Toronto Marlboros defeated the Boston Bruins, 4-1 in the fourth Hall of Fame game. Gross proceeds for the benefit game totalled $2,785.00—minus $300 to Queen's rink, $141.10 for hotel accommodation, $27.50 for taxis and $106.20 for liquor. If nothing else the Kingston hosts were sociable and convivial.

At a meeting in Kingston City Hall before the game, "four of the most influential men in hockey'—New York's Patrick, Boston's Art Ross, Montreal's Leo Dandurand, and NHL President Campbell—met Sutherland and 20 local officials at Kingston City Hall and took steps to rectify the shrine's "too low" financial goal. The four governors, on Patrick's urging, decided to expand their board from nine to 16 members and to establish a separate selection committee "to choose the greats of hockey to be enshrined."

Patrick also recommended that old-time stars be selected soon because "greatness lives on in the memory of fewer and fewer each year." Art Ross disagreed. He said interest could only be maintained by electing greats who are well known to the followers of the sport. Campbell stressed the necessity of dissociating Kingston from the selection of names of those to be enshrined. "If the International Hall of Fame is to be successful, the persons selected in it must be fully worthy and their selection must be beyond controversy." Capt. Sutherland assured the group that Kingston at no time intended to interfere with the selection of honor-roll members.

If the International Hall of Fame is to be successful, the persons selected in it must be fully worthy and their selection must be beyond controversy.

Concerned over financial matters, Sutherland got solid support from one of his former Kingston

Frontenac players: "The solid foundation has been laid by you," Bike Young told his old coach. "So by all means let the big money boys take over with as much coin as they desire to donate." He accepted donations large and small, including $54.00 donated by Kingston City Hockey League on the occasion of his 54th wedding anniversary. The local hockey executives complimented the Captain for his "Never flagging efforts for the advancement of hockey." The Hall's Kingston committee at its annual meeting recognized his contribution in securing the shrine for the city and in keeping the organization "alive and vigorous."

Two months later, at the CAHA's annual meeting in Toronto, Sutherland reported that the Hall of Fame's building fund had reached $55,000, five thousand more than the original objective but because of rising building costs the goal had elevated to $150,000. He then called on Hall of Fame governor George Dudley to present the honor roll scroll to builder Claude C. Robinson of Winnipeg, regarded as the founder of the CAHA. In one of the few recorded acceptance speeches of the era—thanks to the association's custom of recording every spoken word, his grateful remarks were preserved for history: "It is hardly necessary for me to say how happy this little presentation makes me feel," he told delegates in the Royal York Hotel.

"Owing more to circumstances than to any particular merit on my part—I just happened to be there at the crucial time I was catapulted into the position where I could get some organization going. Hockey has been very good to me. Any contribution that I have made to hockey has been a labour of love and I hope I shall be spared for a few more years to enjoy them with you. Thank you very much."

Sutherland's spirit glowed early in June when the NHL clubs underwrote a subscription of $30,000—an average of $5,000 a team—"for the construction of a suitable building"

Sutherland's spirit glowed early in June when the NHL clubs underwrote a subscription of $30,000—an average of $5,000 a team—"for the construction of a suitable building" and launched an architectural design competition for the structure. A month later he was wrapped in gloom. Stuart Crawford, the Hall's president and mayor of Kingston, died unexpectedly. "I found him to be a charming gentleman…a real man's man," Patrick told Sutherland. "I'm sure he'll be sorely missed." It was a understatement, for some critics said his passing dealt a severe blow to the

Kingston Hall of Fame initiative.

Kingston hockey official kept up a brave face. "Subscriptions to the Hall's building fund now total over $47,000, about $3,000 short of the original objective," R.J. Rodden, the shrine's publicity director wrote in the 1948 NHL Guide. "Officials, in view of rising costs of construction, have recently raised their goal to $75,000, a sum which they are confident will be donated within the year. It is anticipated erection of the shrine will begin in the spring."

With his mind on money matters, Capt. Sutherland took little notice of a book published by eminent Maritime author Thomas H. Raddall in 1948. Entitled *Halifax, Warden of the North*, one of the final chapters closed with this bold statement: "It is a fact little known in Canada…that ice-hockey, Canada's national game, began on the Dartmouth Lakes in the eighteenth century. Here garrison officers found the Indians playing a primitive form of hurley on the ice, adopted and adapted it, and later put the game on skates."

Kingston's captain had already conceded the early contribution of the eastern military city in his 1942 "Origin Hockey in Canada" report to the CAHA. The "guns" of the citadel city would not remain silent, but Sutherland was not ready to give an inch on where the Hockey Hall of Fame should be located. And he kept up his relentless campaign and focused on a new outreach.

(Bottom) A key supporter of Captain Sutherland was Alderman Stuart Crawford, who went on to wear the historic chain of office of the Mayor of the City of Kingston. He died unexpectedly and the Hall of Fame movement sputtered.

(Right) N.A. Mervyn ("Red") Dutton (right), former manager of the New York Americans, became National Hockey League president in 1943 and favoured deferring the birthplace debate until after the Second World War. Three years later, Clarence S. Campbell (left), succeeded him as head of the NHL and supported the Kingston bid for a hockey hall of fame.

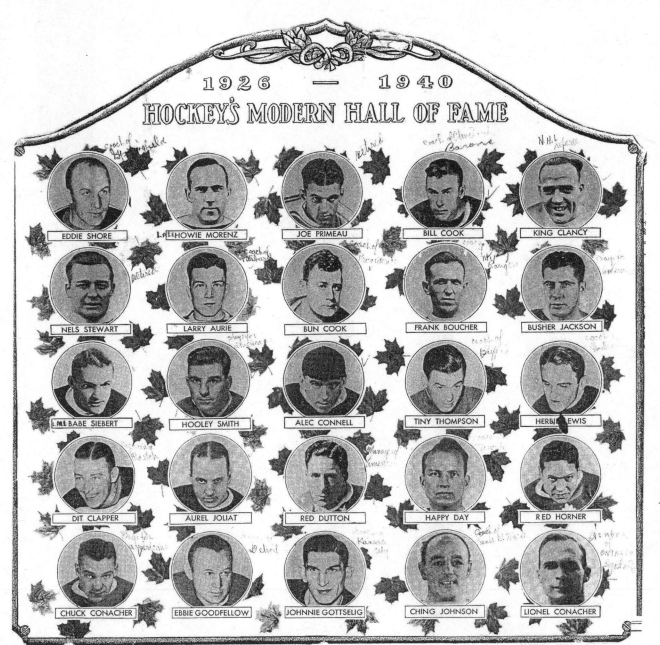

1926 — 1940

HOCKEY'S MODERN HALL OF FAME

EDDIE SHORE HOWIE MORENZ JOE PRIMEAU BILL COOK KING CLANCY

NELS STEWART LARRY AURIE BUN COOK FRANK BOUCHER BUSHER JACKSON

BABE SIEBERT HOOLEY SMITH ALEC CONNELL TINY THOMPSON HERBIE LEWIS

DIT CLAPPER AUREL JOLIAT RED DUTTON HAPPY DAY RED HORNER

CHUCK CONACHER EBBIE GOODFELLOW JOHNNIE GOTTSELIG CHING JOHNSON LIONEL CONACHER

NHL stars shone brightly when there were only six to ten teams active. Between 1926 and 1940, 25 players were cited in a calendar for Hockey's Modern Hall of Fame. Only two, Detroit's Laurie Aurie and Chicago's Johnny Gottselig, were not formally chosen.

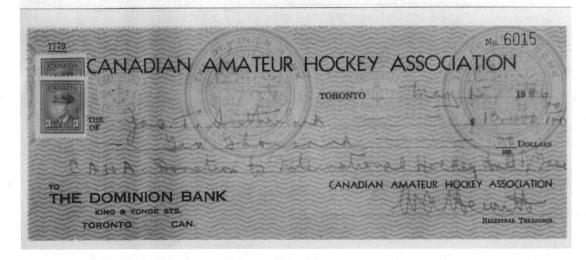

(Opposite page) James Sutherland was proud of the fact that NHL president Clarence Campbell's second Christian name was "Sutherland," and sat beside the new NHL president when Boston Bruins played in a Hall of Fame fundraiser at Kingston's Jock Harty Arena.

(This page) During the 1945-46 fundraising campaign, the National Hockey League and the Canadian Amateur Hockey Association signed cheques payable to the Hall of Fame founder, Capt. Sutherland. The NHL contributed $7,500 as part of its $30,000 pledge but reneged on the $22,500 balance. The amateur CAHA topped the NHL by contributing $10,000. Years later in 1960, Gordon W. Juckes and Jack Roxborough, executive members of the Canadian Amateur Hockey Association, attempted to recover the organization's $10,000 grant to the Kingston project.

James Sutherland contributed to the efforts of the OHA and CAHA to standardize the rules of the game, from early in the century until later in his life. He was respected as an accomplished coach who played by the book.

J.W. Sutherland.

1935 OFFICIAL

HOCKEY RULES

CANADIAN AMATEUR HOCKEY ASSOCIATION

 CONSTITUTION BY-LAWS AND REGULATIONS

RULES GOVERNING ALLAN CUP AND O.H.A. MEMORIAL TROPHY GAMES

PLAYING RULES OF THE GAME

ORGANIZED AT OTTAWA, DECEMBER 4TH, 1914
AMENDED TO OCTOBER, 1934

This International

Hockey Roll of Honor

Has been dedicated to perpetuate the memories of the men who have done so much to develop Nationally and Internationally Canada's Great Winter Sport

This Book also designates the names of the Leagues and Associations that have offered their approval of such a Memorial being designed for this purpose

The National Hockey League

The Canadian Amateur Hockey Association
.. British Columbia Amateur Hockey ,,
.. Alberta Amateur Hockey Assn.
.. Saskatchewan Amateur Hockey Assn
.. Manitoba Amateur Hockey Assn.
.. Thunder Bay Amateur Hockey Assn.
.. Ontario Hockey Association
.. Ottawa & District Amateur Hockey Assn.
.. Quebec Amateur Hockey Assn.
.. Maritime Amateur Hockey Assn.
.. American Hockey Assn. of United States
.. American Hockey League
.. Amateur Hockey Assn. of the United States
.. International Ice Hockey Assn.

Capt. Sutherland conceived the idea of a Roll of Honour and hired a Kingston artist to illuminate the feats of the Hall of Fame nominees. He lugged the 19-pound, seal skin-bound book to Montreal and Boston and showed it off at special events to promote the Kingston project. An alphabetical selection of players and builders follows.

Aubrey Victor Clapper

Aubrey Victor Clapper: Born in Newmarket, Ontario. February 9th 1907. Height, 6 feet, weight 198 pounds, right hand shot.

Aubrey "Dit" Clapper in the fall of 1927, then 19 years old, joined the Boston Bruins Club of the National Hockey League and played his first game November 15th 1927.

He played 20 consecutive seasons as a member of the Boston Club, until his retirement as a player, February 12th 1947. Clapper played in over 850 games for the Bruins, scored 241 goals and 265 assists for a total of 506 points, playing eleven years at right wing and nine years on defense. He played on three Boston Stanley Cup Teams, 1929, 1939, and 1941.

He won the complete respect of friend and foe for his outstanding sportsmanship, and as a man and a player brought honor and fame to the game of hockey, his club, and the city he represented.

Contributed by
Frank Ryan
Boston, Mass.

Allan M. "Scotty" Davidson
A Champion of Champions

Among those greats whose names will hang in hockey's International Hall of Fame none are more deserving and none more admired than that of the dynamic and heroic Allan "Scotty" Davidson; one of Kingston's ice immortals. "He saw a light; he followed it. And e'en his life he yields. He gave his all at duty's call; He rests in Flanders' Fields."

Although many years have passed since "Scotty" Davidson sparked the Toronto professionals to the winning of the Stanley Cup, memories of his amazing deeds are still a vivid green and there are qualified observers who maintain that he was the greatest of them all. Versatile to a marked degree he was equally effective and brilliant on the defence or forward line and a stand-out performer at home or abroad.

Scotty's thrilling career was, alas, cut short by fate but he willed unto the future memories of accomplishment never surpassed in the annals of Canada's national winter sport. As a boy in Portsmouth he was a hockey prodigy and later as a flaming member and Captain of the Kingston O.H.A. Frontenac juniors of 1910-11, he won his golden spurs.

It was more by accident than design that "Scotty" became a professional after playing for one season in Western Canada senior ranks. Eddie Livingstone, a reformer in professional hockey thought, turned to youth in seeking to break the Ottawa-Montreal strangle-hold on Stanley Cup pursuits and thus to Toronto were lured the most promising youngsters in the land, among them Frank Nighbor, Jack Walker and "Scotty" Davidson.

Then almost overnight a great light dawned as the onrushing Torontos smashed long accepted convictions to smithereens and none among the dynamiters was more colorful and destructive than "Scotty Davidson, the most versatile of them all. The Torontos fittingly captured the Stanley Cup in the season of 1914 and Davidson was the outstanding performer in the series. But war came to a startled world in mid-summer and Davidson, who had so much to live for and also with financial security beckoning to him gallantly marched into the maelstrom despite the fact he had a presentiment that he would not return. "He saw a light; He carried on; With firm and gallant stride; God rest him merry, gentlemen. Remember him with pride".

Contributed by
Mike Rodden
Sports Editor
Whig-Standard
Kingston, Ontario.

Charles R. "Chuck" Gardiner

Charles Robert "Chuck" Gardiner born in Edinburgh, Scotland was one of Hockey's greatest goal-keepers when he died in St. Boniface hospital June 13th 1934, aged 30.

He crammed considerable fame into life, won the Vezina trophy twice and helped Chicago Black Hawks win the Stanley Cup in 1934.

Came to Winnipeg from Scotland, first played hockey with school team, played minor hockey with Assiniboines and Winnipeg Tigers; Selkirk seniors in 1925.

Turned pro with Winnipeg Maroons 1927, sold to Chicago Black Hawks 1928, also adept at football and baseball, he was married, — his son Bobbie is a goalie.

Contributed by
Major Abbie Coo
Winnipeg Free Press

Frank McGee

Frank McGee, was the renowned centre of the Ottawa Silver Seven from 1903 to 1906. — During his senior and Stanley Cup career he had the use of only one eye.

McGee is best remembered for his scoring feats, and for setting up the all time Stanley Cup record of fourteen goals in one game. He achieved this feat while playing against Dawson City in 1904.

He was killed on the Somme in 1916. — In addition to being a great hockey player, he was an outstanding rugbyist with Ottawa College and Ottawa City, — and a fine all-round sportsman.

Contributed by
Bazil O'Meara
Sports Editor
Montreal Star

Howie Morenz

His glittering speed made him famous, he lived for speed, at the end, speed took its toll in death, and, perhaps, that is the end that Howie Morenz would have chosen, to die in action, in the midst of the swift rush of the game he loved. Howie Morenz catapulted from an intermediate team at Stratford into the National League, into whose narrow confines was crowded the cream of Canada's hockey stars, he not only crashed into this star studded realm, he had stolen stardom in a few weeks from the established greats, and was quickly termed the Stratford streak. Then it developed that he was born in the little town of Mitchell, he naturally became the Mitchell Meteor. He was also known as the Canadien Comet, the Hurtling Habitant, anything to signify speed — which whirled him through the toughest defence, and against some of the greatest goalers the game has ever known.

The night of Jan. 28th Morenz was in the midst of the most courageous come-back efforts hockey has ever known. He had been sold to Chicago Black Hawks, then to the New York Rangers, but when Cecil Hart had returned to manage Canadiens in 1936 his first official act was to secure his beloved friend Howie from the Rangers, and Howie was back home again.

Canadiens were playing Black Hawks that night — Morenz dashed down right wing, side-stepping Earl Siebert, he tripped, and went crashing into the boards, he was thrown side-ways from the force of his charge, by the very speed that had made him famous, his leg snapped, he died in hospital from complications that ensued, on March 8th 1937.

Thousands attended his funeral service in the Forum, where

so often he had thrilled the crowds. In his first year in the National League 1924 he spear-headed the Canadiens into the World title, as they roared through three great title teams, Ottawa, Vancouver and Calgary in turn, Morenz scored 270 goals in twelve and a half seasons, his speed dazzled the hockey world.

He was a grand sportsman, who never engaged in a fight in his entire career — though he was a hard-driving, gallant and fearless player, he was like a high strung thoroughbred, with a warm personality, a loveable boy with a million friends.

Beloved and respected by his opponents, he became one of the great traditions of hockey in life, and unforgettable in death.

Contributed by
Elmer W. Ferguson
Sports Editor
Montreal Herald

Frank Nighbor
The Pembroke Peach and Super Hockey Star of his era

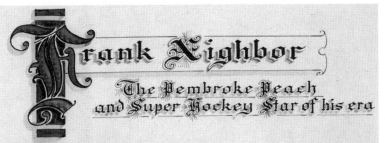

Born in Pembroke, Ontario. January the 25th. 1893. Height 5'11" weight 165 pounds, left hand shot and known as the Pembroke Peach and Super Hockey Star of his era.

Frank started hockey with Debating Team in Pembroke and was transferred to Port Arthur in 1911. Played in Thunder Bay League.

Started Professional Hockey in Toronto in 1912. was drafted to the Coast in 1913 with Vancouver Millionaires, won Stanley Cup in Vancouver in 1914. Came to Ottawa in 1915, was on four Stanley Cup Teams with Ottawa Senators. 1920, 1921, 1923 and 1927. Went to Toronto in 1930. finishing professional hockey as a player. Winner of Hart Trophy for most valuable player in 1923. Winner of Lady Byng Trophy in 1925 and 1926 for most valuable player and least number of penalties.

Coached Buffalo Bisons for five years winning championship in the International League in 1932 and 1933.

Contributed by
Dave Behan
Pembroke, Ont.

Harvey Pulford

Harvey Pulford was outstanding as a defenceman with Ottawas for ten years. He was particularly effective playing for the Silver Seven from 1902 to 1907.

Pulford was considered the greatest all-around player of his time in Canada.

In addition to his greatness as a hockey player, he was a fine football wingman, a great oarsman, paddler and squash player.

In the opinion of many old timers — he was the greatest all-arounder in the history of Canadian sport, — a veritable titan on and off the playing fields.

Contributed by
Bazil O'Meara
Sports Editor
Montreal Star

Captain George Taylor Richardson

One of Canada's most brilliant amateur hockey players and heroic gentlemen

On the morning of August 4th 1914 He was in Quebec City, and in passing in front of the Daily Chronicle newspaper office, just as they were hanging out the morning bulletin board, advising the public that "England was at war with Germany" turning to his companion, Richardson said "That means me". Reaching his home in Kingston the brilliant hockey star of Queen's University and Kingston Frontenacs, proceeded to Military Headquarters, and signified his intention to proceed overseas, and so, accompanied by that other outstanding Kingston player Allan M. "Scotty" Davidson, (whom it is claimed was the first professional hockey player to enlist for overseas service) they proceeded to Valcartier Que. and in due course proceed Overseas with the first 33,000 of "all ranks".

Richardson was a man of outstanding wealth, and held a commission in the famous 14th Princess of Wales Own Rifles, of Kingston. It has been stated by the Lawyer who drew up his will in Valcartier that assured him that he had no expectation whatever of ever seeing Canada again. And so it came to pass, that on a full moonlit night, someone blundered, and sent Richardson and his companions "Over the Top", unfortunately that blunder resulted in being the "last chapter" of one of the finest types of Canadian manhood, that ever wore a pair of skates or shouldered a rifle.

The Richardson Stadium erected to the memory of his gallant brother, and the Richardson public bathing edifice, also the C.A.H.A. Junior Eastern Canada championship Trophy, all donated by his brother the late James A. Richardson, former Chancellor of Queen's University, all stand to-day to testify to the greatness of that worthy hockeyist whose name will ever live on in the glorious records of the International Hall of Fame. Certainly a most worthy selection.

Contributed by
George S. Dudley. K.C.
Secretary-Manager C.A.H.A.
Midland, Ontario.

Edward William Shore

Super Star and Dynamic Defenseman

Born at Fort Qu'Appele – Cupar, Saskatchewan, Nov. 25th 1902. Weight 185, pounds, Right hand shot. Hockey, catering to speed and thrills, has produced so many remarkable and colorful performers that in order to distinguish some from others slightly less gifted, Lester Patrick called the greatest of them "super-stars" and thus partially solved an entrancing riddle. And so it came to pass that one of the first to be so honored was Eddie Shore, former super defenceman with the Edmonton Eskimos and the mighty Boston Bruins.

Truly it can be said that Eddie Shore was a dynamic "Babe" Ruth of the hockey lanes and that in this fascinating sport he had the touch of a Midas-like genius. As a forward he had been an unknown member of the Melville amateurs and he had been tried out by the Vancouver Millionaires and traded by the owners of the Regina Club.

Good fortune placed him on the Edmonton defence and almost over-night the news flashed around the hockey world that a dazzling new star had appeared in a league that catered to many of the sport's most glamorous immortals.

When the Western Canada League broke on the shoals of adversity in 1926 Shore's services were sold to Boston and it was with the Bruins that the man from Qu'Appele – Cupar, Saskatchewan roared to the dizziest heights. And in the staid east where so many stars had shone, many worshipped at the shrine of Shore and called him the greatest of them all.

A man of iron, Shore served with the Bruins for four-teen amazing campaigns and then performed with the New York Americans for part of one season.

FREDERICK WELLINGTON TAYLOR
M.O.B.E.
The "Cyclone" of Canada's National Winter Sport

Born in Tara, Ontario, June 23rd 1883. Moved to Listowel, Ont. at age of 6 where he played Junior, Intermediate and Senior O.H.A. Hockey from 1899 to 1904. Played 1904-5 in Thessalon, Ont., and part 1905-06 at Portage la Prairie, Senior Manitoba League. Turned Professional with Portage Lake Club of Houghton, Michigan in 1906 and played following season, 1906-07 with same club. Won League championship both seasons. Moved to Ottawa, Ont., for the 1907-08 season and played there 1908-09, 1910-11 and 1911-12. Played for Renfrew, Ont., "Millionaires" in 1909-10. Employed by the Dominion Government, Taylor was transferred to Vancouver, B.C. in the fall of 1912 and played all of his hockey thereafter with the Vancouver "Maroons" until he retired at the end of 1921 season.

Known to all hockeydom as the "Cyclone," Taylor enjoyed super-all-star rating from 1903 until his retirement. Believed by many to be the greatest crowd-pleaser and most spectacular player that the game has produced. Converted from colorful defence player to sensational scoring centre, Taylor led all scorers in the Pacific Coast League on 6 occasions.

Fred "Cyclone" Taylor is superintendent in charge of Canadian Immigration activities for all British Columbia and lives with his family in Vancouver, B.C. He is revered and respected as a gentleman and sportsman of the highest calibre and as one who has brought honour and fame to his adopted City and Province as well as to Canada and himself.

Contributed by
Lester Patrick
Madison Square Garden
New York, N.Y.

Georges Vezina

In the early days of Hockey, it was the fashion for the teams to go on barn-storming trips each season, there was no elaborate Stanley Cup games, because it had not acquired the glamour that comes with age.

So at the end of their first season in hockey the Montreal Canadiens went barn-storming, one of their games was played in Chicoutimi, Quebec, that town didn't have much of a hockey team; Canadiens, a great galaxy of atheletes headed by Newsy Lalonde, Pitre, Laviolette and other great stars, could skate rings around the home boys, and out-stick-handle them, but they couldn't score goals because there was a tall, poker-faced youngster in the nets, who just couldn't be beaten.

The late Joe Cattarinich who later became owner of Canadiens, was in the nets for the French team. Joe knew a goaler when he saw one, he asked the name of this gangling youngster, and they told him the boy's name was Georges Vezina, so when George Kennedy acquired the Canadiens he signed Vezina on Cattarinich's recommendation, and Vezina remained the permanent goaler, building himself into a tradition of hockey for fifteen years.

Vezina died, pratically in harness, he was in the nets for Canadiens the night of Nov. 28th 1925, he looked weak and ill, in the dressing room after the first period, a burst of arterial blood spurted from his mouth, it was a forewarning of tuberculosis, and on March 24th 1926, Georges Vezina died at his Chicoutimi home.

Vezina was one of the all-time hockey greats in the nets, off the ice he was quiet, almost to the point of taciturnity, he did not speak English fluently, but that did not matter, he merely

Sir Montague Allan C.V.O.

Donor of

The Allan Cup

Emblematic of
The Senior Amateur Championship of Canada

Shortly after the Stanley Cup became the championship trophy of the Professional Hockey Leagues, Mr. William Northey of Montreal prevailed upon Sir Montague Allan to offer a Trophy for the encouragement of the Amateurs, this occured in 1908.

The Cup was first presented by Sir Montague to the Victorias of Montreal, whose league championship was won by the Cliffsides of Ottawa.

The Queen's University team of Kingston were the first challengers, and were successful in winning the inaugural series of matches for it's possesion.

At the formation of the Canadian Amateur Hockey Association in 1914 the "Allan Cup" was accepted as the trophy emblematic of the senior amateur hockey championship of Canada, under the rules and regulations as enacted by the trustees of the Cup and in accordance with the Deed of Trust. In 1928 the Allan Cup was donated outright to the Canadian Amateur Hockey Association.

Frank Calder

one of the

Builders of Hockey

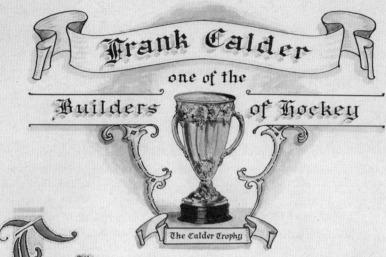

The Calder Trophy

Frank Calder is the man who died for hockey, the man who gave his life for the game he loved, with an amazing fervour ...amazing because he never played hockey, and, as a boy, never saw hockey, but established his first contacts with the whirlwind game in the capacity of a sports writer doing his regular chores of keeping his shoulders brushing against the news.

Frank Calder was secretary of the National Hockey Association for several years before that organisation was disbanded. The National Hockey League was formed in November 1917. He was elected president then, of the new war-baby of sport that launched a timorous course on a stormy sea. He was still President, and hockey's ship was plunging wildly in the stormy seas of another world war, when on February 4th 1943, he died quietly. He died within a stone's throw of the Montreal Forum, which was built originally to stage the games of his League. He died with his portfolio spread on his bed, ready to transact the business of the League.

John Ross Robertson
one of the

Builders of Hockey

The J. Ross Robertson Cup

John Ross Robertson was not a charter member of the Ontario Hockey Association but like everything else with which he came into contact he left an indelible impression on the game. And during his six years of leadership it really became Canada's National Sport. Mr. Robertson when he was induced to assume the presidency was one of the really great Canadians.

Founder of the Toronto Evening Telegram, he had built up that marvellous monument to his memory, the Hospital for Sick Children. Was Member of Parliament for East Toronto and had refused a knighthood.

All of these things were typical of his bigness and when he stepped into the field of hockey as an avocation he brought to bear all the traits that had made him an outstanding figure in the world of philanthropy of business and of politics.

Arthur Howey "Art" Ross
Super-Hockey Star
Brilliant Executive
and Inventive Genius

Hockey owes to Arthur Howey "Art" Ross a greater debt of gratitude than perhaps those in hockey today realize. The debt is two-fold, as a player Ross contributed many brilliant and colorful chapters to the game when it was in its infancy as a professional sport, historic feats of skill that helped lay the foundation for hockey's present greatness.

As a leader and executive Arthur Ross was even greater importance than his athletic feats. He spear-headed the eastern invasion of professional hockey from Canada into the United States, when in 1924 he accepted the leadership of the Boston Club, in a city to which professional hockey was a new and almost unknown game, making its first appearance south of the border in the east, in that difficult capacity Arthur Ross laid a firm and lasting corner-stone, as with infinate patience overcoming many disappointments he assembled one great team after another, teams which included many of the hockey greats of modern times.

Boston has become one of the staunch pillars of the National Hockey League, a city in which hockey, from a humble start in a small rink has assumed the proportions of a major game. In 1924 the owners of the Boston Club were the first to realize the pontentialities of hockey as a sports attraction in the major American cities of the east.

QUITE A GUY!—Scroll calls Art Ross "super-hockey star, brilliant executive, and inventive genius." Presentation is by James B. Garvin, president of hockey's Hall of Fame. *Dec. 4, 1949*

Art Ross's contributions to hockey as a player, manager, and goal net designer were acknowledged with his induction into the Hall of Fame.

Roll of Honour

Arthur Howey "Art" Ross
Super-Hockey Star
Brilliant Executive
and Inventive Genius

Hockey owes to Arthur Howey "Art" Ross a greater debt of gratitude than perhaps those in hockey today realize. The debt is two-fold, as a player Ross contributed many brilliant and colorful chapters to the game when it was in its infancy as a professional sport, historic feats of skill that helped lay the foundation for hockey's present greatness.

As a leader and executive Arthur Ross was even greater importance than his athletic feats. He spear-headed the eastern invasion of professional hockey from Canada into the United States, when in 1924 he accepted the leadership of the Boston Club, in a city to which professional hockey was a new and almost unknown game, making its first appearance south of the border in the east, in that difficult capacity Arthur Ross laid a firm and lasting corner-stone, as with infinate patience overcoming many disappointments he assembled one great team after another, teams which included many of the hockey greats of modern times.

Boston has become one of the staunch pillars of the National Hockey League, a city in which hockey, from a humble start in a small rink has assumed the proportions of a major game. In 1924 the owners of the Boston Club were the first to realize the pontentialities of hockey as a sports attraction in the major American cities of the east.

When Lester Patrick was inducted into the Kingston hall during a game in New York, Capt. Sutherland donned a tux and joined Brigadier General J.R. Kilpatrick in extending congratulations. "The Silver Fox" was a prime supporter of the Kingston project and lauded the Captain as "The Connie Mack of Hockey."

"You can now add to your list of accomplishments that of a leading performer in a motion picture." —NHL President Clarence S. Campbell, Letter to Capt. James T. Sutherland, December 28, 1948.

FRONT AND CENTRE

(1948-1952)

1. HOCKEY'S CAVALCADE

At age 78, Capt. Sutherland had a long list of credits to his name as a player, coach, manager, administrator, salesman, author, broadcaster, and creator of a sports museum initiative. Five years had passed since North America's leading hockey bodies had granted the Hall of Fame to his hometown of Kingston but the shrine had not yet materialized. As spiritual leader of the proposed Hall of Fame, he had joined other immortals formally honoured in the mythical building. Then he had suffered a setback in the loss of the organization's political and business leader in the death of Stuart Crawford.

As 1948 faded into history, the imperturbable septuagenarian received a welcome pickup. He was advised that "an educational film on the development of hockey," in which he had played a prominent role, would soon to be released to the public. It had been filmed six months earlier by Associated Screen News depicting an early Kingston game, in front of Kingston City Hall with the 1846 Martello (Shoal) Tower in the background. A crowd of 300 persons watched as Max Jackson's Junior B Vics, wearing mid-19th century Malabar costumes and carrying short, curved sticks re-enacted an early game on Kingston harbour ice.

Although players carried replicas of sticks used in the 1880s games between Queen's and Royal Military colleges, they wore military uniforms similar to those worn by British soldiers in the 1840s. This fitted Sutherland's vision of the origin of the game as related in the CAHA Origins report. Intentionally or inadvertently, the film, entitled "Hockey's Cavalcade," strengthened the Kingston legend of the game's beginnings.

Intentionally or inadvertently, the film, entitled "Hockey's Cavalcade," strengthened the Kingston legend of the game's beginnings.

The announcement of the film stirred up quite a discussion among the CAHA's minor hockey committee members on what would be most beneficial to young players. Rather than being a history of hockey, some officials felt it would be better to produce a series of short films designed to demonstrate body checking, tripping, and boarding. Sutherland agreed, but no other film idea ever reached Canadian movie screens.

The Captain went back to Kingston and his main concern—a suitable site for hockey's first shrine. In mid-1949, the local committee asked for a site at Stuart and Barrie streets, next to the Frontenac County Courthouse. President Campbell was already on record as opposing the Hall site at the Kingston Fairgrounds Community Memorial Centre. "I hope you will not think I am unreasonably unsympathetic to your point of view," Campbell told Sutherland. "I know how much this institution means to you and I would not have any more fervent wish in respect to it then that you should see it brought to fruition and I am confident that you will but it must be done with a view to getting the maximum results for the funds and nothing that is slipshod will be of any use so far as I am concerned."

Campbell also weighed in on the debate as to who should be enshrined and ensured Sutherland that his two favourite ex-Frontenacs, George Richardson and Scotty Davidson —in his estimation "the two greatest hockey players ever to lace up skates"—would be given full consideration." The rules of selection, he advised, had been discussed with Ross and Patrick, but he did not have full approval of the Board of Governors—"partly due to oversight and some to neglect."

In spite of such notable induction events and a building fund that neared $60,000 as 1950 dawned, Sutherland and colleagues still had to defend Kingston's birthplace title.

October 1949, Magistrate James B. Garvin, the new president of the Kingston Hall, announced two new members: Art Ross—"possessor of one of the most inventive minds in hockey," and Winnipeg Victoria's D.H. (Danny) Bain, cited as one of the fastest skaters of the 1890s. The latter, a vigorous, 75-year-old sportsman, learned of his election to the Hall while on a duck hunting trip in Manitoba. Two months later, with Sutherland among the 350 friends and hockey luminaries at Boston's Hotel Statler, Ross's election was celebrated as he completed 25 years as manager of the Bruins. He received an illuminated scroll saluting him as a "super-hockey star, brilliant executive and inventive genius." *The Boston Globe*'s Herb Ralby described him as "one of the greatest if not the greatest personality hockey has ever known." Local hockey writers and radio commentators presented "Uncle Arthur" with a solid gold cigarette case. Campbell gave him a silver tray decorated with the insignias of the six clubs. More silver came from "The Gallery Gods," the faithful fans from the upper regions of Boston Garden.

In spite of such notable induction events and a building fund that neared $60,000 as 1950 dawned, Sutherland and colleagues still had to defend Kingston's birthplace title. "There is even today some reluctance to accept Kingston as the native home of hockey," Vince Lunny wrote in *The Montreal Standard*. This quotation was repeated in a British book, *Ice Hockey*, by Robert Giddens, a Montreal ex-patriot who played hockey in England and became editor of *Ice Hockey World*. In a six-page chapter on "The Origin," he reviewed the birthplace debate dating back to Menke and declared: "After much deliberation and after grave and careful consideration to all arguments put forth, it was decided to accept Kingston, Ontario as the traditional home of Canada's great game." He added this point: "There seems little doubt that Montreal was the centre of the game's practical beginning."

In his concluding paragraph, Giddens dutifully focused on ice hockey's Old World roots, from which ice hockey sprouted, grew, and flourished: "The Greeks, the Irish, the Danes, the Swedes and many more countries who have fashioned a game on variations of the stick and ball game have all built stepping stones which led to a comparative new game—Canadian ice hockey—a rugged, manly, spectacularly fast game played by aggressive, restless and colourful Canadians."

3. CAMPBELL'S COMING

Despite minor differences and criticisms, James Sutherland and Clarence Campbell marched together to inch the Hall project ahead. In September 1950, the NHL president drove to Kingston on a twin mission to support the city's quest for a new arena as well as to promote a hockey shrine. Introduced by Gus Marker, a NHL veteran living in Kingston, Campbell addressed the Kiwanis Club on "The Value of Sport to Individuals and Communities" and took time to thank Sutherland "who conceived the idea for the rink and the hall of fame." After the luncheon, he inspected the site for the building and gave his approval.

Heartened by the decision, Sutherland went back to promoting his pet project. He wrote and distributed a pamphlet listing the 18 players and seven builders honored to date. The latter number grew to nine later, when the new edition of Menke's *All-Sports Record Book* was published. It contained the names of two donors of the game's most prestigious trophies: Lord Stanley of Preston and Sir Montagu Allan of Montreal.

We are perhaps a little overzealous in talking about hockey," he concluded, "but just as the United States of America believes in its baseball superiority, we in Canada feel that hockey is a game were are entitled to be very happy about.

On October 10, 1950, Sutherland celebrated his 80th birthday, gave up the chair as president of the Kingston City League, and was named a life member. Other matters were uppermost in Sutherland's mind—the Frontenac County Courthouse site was "approved" by County Council. Earlier in the year, he had confessed to Campbell "that nothing else has occupied my brain for at least 60 percent of my waking and insomnia efforts to sleep." The great obstacle checking the councillors' "spirit of liberality," said Sutherland, was that the proposed Hall would detract from the viewpoint of the west end of the prestigious courthouse that overlooked the Cricket Field and historic City Park.

Publicly, he was optimistic about the long delayed

project. In a radio broadcast, which was recorded for posterity by CKWS Kingston, he predicted a construction start in the spring of 1951 and invited listeners to visit the shrine and see how players were honoured. "We are perhaps a little overzealous in talking about hockey," he concluded, "but just as the United States of America believes in its baseball superiority, we in Canada feel that hockey is a game were are entitled to be very happy about."

Impatient with the process and opposed to having a design competition among architects, Sutherland received discouraging words from Campbell just before Christmas 1950. The NHL president advised against "immediate construction in view of world conditions and the priority for materials" being established by all governments. "Added to this difficulty is the fact that currents costs to build are such that no one builds anything today that is not absolutely essential." Campbell followed up this with another missive: "No one could describe the Hall of Fame as an essential structure at this time, and I think we would alienate the support of a great many people whose support is necessary if the project is to be a real success."

3. GROWING MEMBERSHIP

With site and building plans still up in the air, "Sutherland and Company" greeted 1951 by honoring three pioneer players between the first and second periods of a NHL game at the Montreal Forum. Admitted to the still homeless hall were former Montreal Vics' player and referee Mike Grant; Quebec's great goal scorer and sportsman Joe Malone; and Edward (Newsy) Lalonde, called "the greatest and most colourful player" of the seven-man era. "No, it can't be so," said the 62-year-old Lalonde was quoted as saying when advised of the honor. It's "great," he added, to join with other immortals of Canada's national winter sport.

Five months later, the Kingston "shrine boosted the number of greats to 36 by announcing the names of six other nominated players." Leading the list were two that especially pleased Sutherland, two members of his championship Kingston Frontenacs—amateur George T. Richardson and Toronto professional Alan (Scotty) Davidson—both of whom gave their lives in the First World War. They were joined by another great amateur, Harry J. Trihey, and prominent professional Graham Drinkwater, both significant names in Montreal hockey history.

Sutherland got strong support from the Hall's treasurer, James de St. Remy, a local car dealer and sponsor of hockey teams. Favouring the County of Frontenac site approved by Campbell, he urged efforts to build in 1951. "Let's make our plans to build...without fail." But there was another high profile project in the city, which Sutherland and a host of citizen-sportsmen favoured—formally entitled "The Kingston Community, Memorial and Health Centre," but basically a new hockey arena, the city's first in 25 years.

On March 15, 1951, Sutherland, the Hall's vice-president Bill Watts, and sportsman Wally Elmer were at centre ice as the new memorial to men who died during the Second World War (1939-1945) was officially opened. They joined 3,100 fans as Ontario Hockey Association president Jack Roxborugh congratulated Kingston on "a job well done" and expressed his admiration for the $750,000 structure. He dropped the puck and the Kingston's Senior B Nylons whipped the Belleville Redmen, 12-4. That accomplished, the Captain and his colleagues concentrated efforts on their other great dream—the Hall of Fame building.

With costs spiralling and the dollar objective now in six figures, the Kingston committee, with support of the NHL, continued fund-raising efforts. In January 1952, Montreal Canadiens sent several stars and nine juniors to face the Kingston All-Stars in an exhibition game at the new arena. NHL President Campbell dropped the ceremonial puck and congratulated Kingston "on such an attractive and modern edifice" before the visitors crushed the locals 16-4. The gate totalled $4,537.15 and raised the Hall of Fame fund to $78,537.15.

The eight-year old project appeared to be given a much needed "verbal shot in the arm" when hockey's top executive spoke to Kingston Lions at the La Salle Hotel. "I share the fervent hope that economic conditions and building costs will soon be such as to enable to have a real edifice in Kingston which will be a landmark...wherein will be the records of those who gave so much to make hockey a great game and made it possible for a hockey player to have such a fine career in whatever community he lives, to be one of its leading citizens." Later, Campbell, in a letter to Secretary St. Remy and Sutherland, reiterated his views on the Kingston project but with a different focus. "It is the opinion of the Governors that a 'suitable building' cannot be financed with the funds available.... and as practical businessmen they feel that it would be folly to construct any building of this type at this time of extremely inflated prices for both labour and materials."

Sutherland, like a dogged politician, kept up his campaigning. At the CAHA annual meeting in Minaki,

Ontario, he reported 25 inductees had been photographed and framed for the proposed shrine and then commented: "I never thought 63 years ago, when I put on a pair of skates and shin pads and played in 1888, I would be appealing for assistance for a hockey hall of fame."

Outside of Kingston, support for the project was sporadic. One voice, former Torontonian Frank J. Selke, spoke up in Montreal. "Some day, someone is going to build the Hall at Kingston," the Canadiens' manager told Ted Reeve of *The Toronto Telegram*. "When that happens, those of us who are still around are going to regret not having done something tangible about preparing an adequate history of the game of hockey which has entertained countless millions and which have been very good to me and others."

Montreal Canadiens sent several stars and nine juniors to face the Kingston All-Stars in an exhibition game at the new arena.

The location in Kingston was still a toss up as the approved site next to the prestigious Frontenac County Courthouse caused a public outcry. Late in 1952, Queen's professor James A. Roy recorded the situation in his popular book, *Kingston, The King's Town*: "Even in this commercial age, many Kingstonians would rather do without the tourists' money than allow the amenities in their city to be tampered with." The shrine was promoted as a revenue source for the city.

Sutherland and cohorts turned to a new/old site. Cooke's United Church on Brock Street in downtown Kingston was offered at the cost of $61,800. The old brick edifice did not meet favour with Campbell (who died in 1984, eight years before the NHL-supported Hockey Hall of Fame moved into a former Bank of Montreal building in downtown Toronto.)

In this still from the Hockey Cavalcade *movie, Captain Sutherland is shown accepting on behalf of the Hockey Hall of Fame a donation of a Japanese vase from a North Battleford, Saskatchewan team that received it during a 1930s Japanese tour.*

For a re-enactment of the historic hockey game, the city's Junior B players donned replica uniforms and portrayed soldiers playing old time hockey in front of an 1840s Martello tower.

With the departure of Sutherland, another James – de St. Remy – took up the torch for the Kingston project. A car dealer and supporter of Kingston hockey team, "The Saint" sought government grants for the still struggling shrine.

Frontenac County Courthouse, which overlooks Kingston's historic City Park and Cricket Field, was approved by County Council as the site of the hall of fame in 1950. Plans were drawn to locate the hall on a corner lot, but a groundswell of opposition from historically-minded citizens quashed the proposal.

The Original Hockey Hall of Fame in Kingston was originally known as the International Hockey Hall of Fame, in recognition of its "CanAm" membership, but grew to include European hockey players and teams. In 1992, an agreement was reached with the International Ice Hockey Federation to have the Kingston shrine become the International Ice Hockey Federation Museum. That partnership was abandoned in 1997 and the Hall became known as the International Hockey Hall of Fame and Museum. The name of the Hall changed again in 2012 to become the Original Hockey Hall of Fame.

Eddie Shore and Frank "King" Clancy greet Captain Sutherland and Stuart Crawford (President of the Hall of Fame) as they display their pages from the Honour Roll.

DELAY OF GAME

(1953-1955)

"Today the Hockey Hall of Fame is no nearer realization than when the first move was made on September 10, 1943." — Vern DeGeer, Montreal, 1953.

1. SHATTERED DREAMS

After 10 years of struggling, he Kingston committee members were far from providing "a priceless memorial" for hockey. Early in 1953, President Campbell told the Canadian Press that the raising of close to $100,000 was insufficient to start construction. Then he set a new goal of $150,000.

Captain Sutherland—still saluted as The Grand Old Man of Hockey—kept his head up and carried on with his dream and his duties. Late in February 1953, he presented a Hall of Fame scroll to Ol' Poison—Nels Stewart—in St. Catharines and mailed a similar citation to the widow of Mickey McKay, "a great player" in the Pacific Coast League and later in the NHL in the 1920s. As to acquiring sufficient building funds and a finding a firm location, the Captain saw little positive news.

The first crack in the Kingston project appeared in January 1953 when Jim Bastable of the Canadian Press wrote a series of three feature articles that were spread across the country in leading daily newspapers. "Hockey Hall of Fame on Rocks of Neglect" blared the heading on the inaugural story. "The ground for the edifice hasn't been broken yet and the bankroll is only $65,000." The second and third articles were more sympathetic to the Hall and to its founder—"Sutherland Made Hockey His Life"—but the damage was done.

Montreal's Vern DeGeer seized on Bastable's key phrase and featured it in a special article wired to the *Detroit Sunday Times*. "It is riding on the rocks of neglect because of the failure of the country's hockey leaders to respond to the plan mapped out by (Captain) Sutherland," said DeGeer. "Today, the land at Kingston donated for the memorial stands untouched. Pictures, old uniforms, and countless articles of hockey equipment, dating back to the days of 'bandy' on the ice, are stored away in the home of shrine founder Sutherland." There had been "talk" of the NHL taking over the administration of the Hall of Fame, he wrote, and declared the shrine is now running into its tenth year of conversation and little action. "Sutherland's dream may become a reality, but at the current pace Jim may not be around," DeGeer added from his Montreal base. "It depends on organized hockey interests."

The head of organized professional hockey was not amused. In fact, Clarence Campbell was quite perturbed and a little bit irked—in his scholarly way—citing Sutherland's comment about "organized hockey doing little about it" and noting that the NHL had given only $7,500 and defaulted on payment of the $30,000 the governors promised. "No matter what is said about the attitude of the National Hockey League in this connection I will always remain a booster for the Hockey Hall of Fame," Campbell wrote to Sutherland in January, 1953. "Some day it will surely be built and it will be a credit to the game and a national shrine for its 'greats'. However, I hardly need to tell you that publicity of the kind…is not calculated to improve the good will of the Governors of the NHL."

Campbell questioned and expressed sorrow that the remarks attributed to Sutherland represented "the official attitude of the Kingston Committee" and cautioned him that newspapermen "don't always interpret anyone's remarks in the manner intended." And with the mind of a considerate juror, he added: "I know where your heart is in this matter and I will do all I can to go along with you, but in doing so I will have to exercise my best judgment as I see it."

The dispute prompted *The Whig-Standard* to present a 1,500-word situation summary under a three-column wide heading: "Hockey Hall of Fame Site Still Here Although Construction Date Unknown."

Written by Murray Kennedy, a junior reporter under Sports Editor Mike Rodden, the article concluded with a Montreal statement that the NHL governors might take the Hall away from Kingston. "NHL governors are not interested in any project except Kingston," Campbell emphatically responded. If they were interested in another project, Kennedy added, "It is not of their power to change the site agreed upon by all the governing bodies of hockey."

"NHL governors are not interested in any project except Kingston," Campbell emphatically responded.

Sutherland soldiered on. At the annual meeting of the CAHA in Niagara Falls, Ontario, in May, 1953, he reported 40 candidates had been photographed and framed with a balance of $65,000 remaining. "It has been a difficult matter to raise this money and I have done all the begging I can," he pleaded. "Let's make this truly a national shrine." Few major donors, including the federal and provincial governments, stepped forward with money and the building fund remained stagnant.

Money matters were uppermost in the mind of the man who was nearing his 83rd birthday but he couldn't shake hockey's historical aspects. In July, he wrote a letter to Baz O'Meara of *The Montreal Star* and opined: "It would do no harm to have all the oldtimers scratching their heads and brushing up on 'Just Where that Darn Old Game of Ours Did Get Started Really.'"

Globe and Mail sports writer W.V. (Bill) Roche attempted that in publishing *The Hockey Book*, containing vignettes from 50 story-telling greats, including Sutherland. "Ice hockey is a Canadian game, conceived and developed by Canadians," he concluded. "It's right at this point at hockey's beginning that arguments started and still continue." Like the birthplace discussion, the Hall of Fame debate roared on.

As the year 1954 arrived, Captain Sutherland and his wife, the former Ethel Mary Metcalfe, posed for a photographer and celebrated their diamond wedding anniversary. The hometown paper summarized his 50-year career as a commercial shoe salesman and concluded: "He is known from one end of Canada to the other for his interest in hockey." That included home and abroad. At the Kingston City League's first annual banquet, the life-long army captain stepped forward and presented the Nelles Megaffin Trophy to the captain of the Kingston Army team, but not before reciting the city's rich hockey history.

Kingston Goodyears, in between two OHA Senior B championship years—1953 and 1954—saluted the "Grand Old Man of Hockey" with a full page spread in their program: "Hats off to the gentleman who has guided the destinies of so many hockey enterprises successfully, one of the greatest living hockey authorities, Capt. James T. Sutherland."

His keenness over national activities as well as local happenings was evidently declining as the Hockey Hall of Fame initiative dragged its skates.

His keenness over national activities as well as local happenings was evidently declining as the Hockey Hall of Fame initiative dragged its skates. Campbell cited this in a letter to Sutherland in September, 1954. "I note your sense of frustration with respect to the major interest of your life," the NHL president sympathized. "Frankly, Jim, I don't have the answer at the moment as to where to secure additional funds necessary for construction of the building, but my experience tells me that $125,000 would be a very inadequate fund to undertake such a project and of course, I have no means of securing it."

Campbell, in his eighth year as NHL president and in the 49th year of his life, had a sympathetic and a positive feeling for the heritage of the game. He commiserated with Sutherland and his cause, and he took time out to attend a unique gathering of pioneer players in Montreal. He broke bread and shared stories with Archie Hodgson, Harlie Routh, Claire MacKerrow, and William Barlow of the MAAA; Gordon Lewis, Mike Grant, and Fred McRobie of Victorias, and Harry Westwick of Ottawa. Organized by Frank Stocking, a former Quebec goaltender, who spoke on the great winter game's development from 1880 to 1900, the event was a forerunner of the oldtimers' hockey movement. The next breach in the Kingston case appeared in May 1955 when Mike Rodden repeated Dink Carroll's allegation that the project "appears to have fallen flat on its face." No building has been purchased, he stated, and souvenirs, such as sticks, skates, and sweaters worn by greats of the past are in storage. A month later the same Montreal writer broke the news that Canadian National Exhibition officials in Toronto planned to establish a general Sports Hall of Fame, including a hockey section.

2. SPORTS HALL OF FAME

The Toronto announcement upset Kingston's "elder statesman of hockey." In a special non-bylined article in *The Gazette*, Sutherland declared the Hall would NOT be situated in Kingston. His dream of establishing a permanent resting place for hockey memorabilia had been dissipated by recent developments. "Certain interests elsewhere have the finances to build and maintain a Hall of Fame," he said without specifying who or where but hinted at the possibility of a shrine being added to McGill University's proposed new arena. He spoke of the lack of co-operation from hockey's governing bodies as a blow to his ambition of establishing a hockey landmark. He announced that he intended to turn over framed pictures, hockey sticks and pucks, "and various other relics of the game" housed in his basement to authorities "when and if a hall of fame is established."

In a special non-bylined article in* The Gazette, *Sutherland declared the Hall would NOT be situated in Kingston.

The Sutherland retreat prompted Campbell to plead with Kingston authorities to stick with their project. "If he finds these articles—of historical interest—a burden and a nuisance in his home, then I think it would do well to spend a little money to have them properly crated and stored," Campbell told Magistrate Garvin, president of the Kingston Hall. There was no public reaction to the story in the Montreal press. A few days later, *The Gazette* carried a photograph of Sutherland and the Hall's Book of Honour, with a telling catch line: "A Shattered Dream."

The Kingston survivors, led by secretary-treasurer James de St. Remy, scurried around for financial support. One possible corporate source—O'Keefe's Brewery—was quickly shot down by Campbell. "I am confident the NHL would not be party to an arrangement in which any beer or spirits' organization is associated." Years later this policy would change and hockey's major league would accept any and all alcohol commercials.

Despite the negative news, the Kingston committee held tight and awaited reports of developments in Toronto. Canada's Sports Hall of Fame was founded at the CNE with 55 members, including three hockey players as inductees—Newsy Lalonde, Howie Morenz and Canada's athlete of the half century, Lionel Conacher. "It is a national scrapbook in which the memory of great Canadian athletes and sporting events is permanently perpetuated," CNE officials proclaimed.

"It will be an all-inclusive Hall of Fame," reported Sutherland's prime supporter in Montreal, Baz O'Meara. The proposal, he conjectured, is to take over the present Hockey Hall, with all those who have been named so far, and incorporate it into Canada's Sports Hall of Fame at Toronto's Exhibition Grounds. "Jim Sutherland's decision to abandon the old hall must have caused some heart wrenching, but it was inevitable," said O'Meara. "No progress was being made, and there seemed to be little interest in the production, or perhaps Kingston as the site of the Hall."

Kingston's Mike Rodden rose to sympathize with his old friend. "It was a long, trying and heart-breaking road that Jim Sutherland travelled," he wrote under his Sports Highways' column banner. "He did, in fact, accomplish more than did all the other members of the executives and committees…But suddenly, after all those years he unwillingly reached the conclusion that his dream would not come true. The city he aimed to serve will be the loser."

Rodden, an alumnus of Queen's University at Kingston, who had spent a score of years in the sports and newspaper business in Toronto, wasn't enthusiastic about the proposed new site for the combined sports hall. He pointed out that Toronto, unlike Montreal, had produced no outstanding sports inventors. "The CNE edifice would be an entity of no historical local value. It would be visited by millions but it could have a hollow sound. Moreover, it and its builders would be held up to scorn, if, by accident, the actual birthplace of hockey is ever discovered—and that is something that isn't likely to happen."

3. DEATH OF THE CAPTAIN

The birthplace debate rambled on and it wasn't long after that Toronto authorities indicated they planned to create a separate shrine for hockey at the CNE. This report had a devastating effect. A dozen weeks after Sutherland's dream appeared shattered, "the grand old man of hockey" died on September 16, 1955, just three weeks short of his 85th birthday. So ended 13 years of fortuitous and frustrating effort for the man who dared dream of a hall of fame for hockey.

A dozen weeks after Sutherland's dream appeared shattered, "the grand old man of hockey" died.

His passing was front page news in Kingston: "Captain Jim Sutherland, Hockey Hero, Dies at 84—Kingstonian's Dream of Building Hall of Fame, Unfulfilled at Death" streamed *The Whig-Standard* headline. In Montreal, where Sutherland provided reams of hockey copy for the press, his death was noted in a three-inch story on the sports pages under a one-column heading: "J. Sutherland, Hockey Hall Founder, Dies." *The Star* played the death of the shrine's founder more prominently with a head and shoulders' photo and a two-column heading that contained "Hall" in quotation marks and this comment: "There is no building such as baseball's Hall of Fame at Cooperstown, N.Y. where the relics may be displayed."

One vital sentence revealed Sutherland had been in ailing health for two years. *The Star*'s sports editor, Baz O'Meara, commented at the bottom of his daily column: "The late Jim Sutherland never realized his ambition of having the Hall built in Kingston. It is probable…that the illness that resulted in his death was emphasized when other auspices decided to admit hockey players into their athletic hall of fame—(i.e. Toronto)." This reiterated what the Canadian Press stated in its wired obituary: "Sutherland's big dream in life was to see some monument erected to the greats of Canada's national winter sport. It never came true probably sparked by news that the shrine would be built in place other than Kingston."

Columnist Rodden led the list of tributes: "Rest easy, Jim, in the valley, because behind you, you have left a heritage that is priceless. In this city and this country you will never be forgotten. Life has begun; not ended."

"Once I am snuffed out, my name will continue, emblazoned on a stone at a very nice place … I will be lying within 50 feet of Sir John A. Macdonald…the first Prime Minister of Canada."

At his funeral, local and national hockey officials presented sincere eulogies and comments. They followed their old comrade to his last resting place in Kingston's historic Cataraqui Cemetery. Many of his associates knew exactly where his body would rest. At the CAHA annual meeting 11 years earlier, Capt. Sutherland—with a great sense of history—recorded the fact during a discussion on the hall of fame project.

"This memorial is not for Sutherland, it is for hockey," he told delegates. "Once I am snuffed out, my name will continue, emblazoned on a stone at a very nice place … I will be lying within 50 feet of Sir John A. Macdonald…the first Prime Minister of Canada." As recorded in CAHA minutes, colleague George Panter of Gravenhurst replied: "I do submit that Sir John would probably consider it a greater honour to be lying within 50 feet of James T. Sutherland."

At the Sutherland gravesite, his granite obelisk contains his full name, plus the name of his wife, who died nine days later. Inscribed above are crossed hockey sticks framed by laurel leaves from the design of the original crest of his beloved Kingston hockey shrine.

PLAYING THE FIELD

By DINK CARROLL

One for the Waste Basket

At a time when everybody is being urged to save paper, a glossy brochure comes out of Kingston whipping up the old argument about the origin of hockey. . . . .

The four-page piece, which appears under the title, "Menke, Misinformed, Misses Hockey Boat," attempts to belittle the value of Frank Menke's work as a sports historian and also takes Prof. E. M. Orlick, of McGill University, for a free ride. Mr. Menke is too firmly established as an international authority on sports to be hurt

McGill professor E.M. Orlick lashed out at the decision to anoint Kingston's bid for the hockey shrine and described it as "the greatest hoax perpetuated in the annals of Canadian sport." Veteran Montreal sports columnist Dink Carroll with the help of a political cartoonist dug up the Hall of Fame issue when it was it appeared dead during the Second World War. He used Frank Menke's arguments to attack Sutherland.

Amid the gloom of the hockey shrine project, James Sutherland and his wife, Ethel, both 84, happily celebrated their diamond-wedding anniversary at their Kingston home in 1954. They posed beside a television set, a service which was new to Canada.

THE KINGSTON WHIG-STANDARD — SATURDAY, JANUARY 30, 1954

CAPT. AND MRS. JAMES T. SUTHER-LAND, who are today celebrating their 60th wedding anniversary, are shown sitting in front of their new television set, the gift of their son and daughter-in-law, Mr. and Mrs. James Sutherland, and their daughter, Mrs. Reginald Dew and Mr. Dew, of Detroit, Mich. Miss Joan Sutherland, Toronto, a granddaughter, arrived during the day.

—Pense

BACK TO THE OLD FIRES!

CAPT. JAMES T. SUTHERLA ARRIVED HOME MONDAY.

He Enlisted in the 146th Four an Half Years Ago—Spent Much T In France.

After four and a half years's ar service, most of which was spent France and England, Staff-Capt "Jim" Sutherland, who went ov eas as Quartermaster of the g old 146th Battalion (Frontena Own) returned to Kingston on M day afternoon.

After the 146th Battalion had be absorbed by a Toronto Battali Capt. Sutherland was appointed S or Quartermaster to the 1st Ca dian Training Battalion, with wh he served until the unit was dem lized. He then became quarterm ter of the 2nd Canadian Comma Depot at Hastings and was appoin from that unit to the staff of Quartermaster-General to act as spector of Ordnance. Capt. Suth land was then stationed at Ramsga (which town claims to have attra ed more Hun bombing raids th any place in England) and when t Canadian units were transferred Buxton, the Captain was transferr

Captain and Mrs. James Sutherland Mark Diamond Wedding Anniversary

Capt. and Mrs. James T. Sutherland, 88 Sydenham street, today observed their diamond wedding anniversary. They were at home to the members of their family and friends. Their only surviving daughter, Mrs. Reginald Dew, (Ethel May) Detroit, Mich., and their son, James, Kingston, were with them.

Capt. and Mrs. Sutherland, who are both 84, were married in St. Paul's Anglican Church by the Rev. Archdeacon W. B. Carey. Mr. Sutherland's parents were also married in St. Paul's church.

Mr. Sutherland has the honor of being a past president and a life member of both the Canadian Amateur Hockey Association, and the Ontario Hockey Association, and is known from one end of Canada to the other for his interest in hockey and other amateur sports. He is the only man in Canada to be a life member of both hockey groups.

Born in Kingston, Oct. 10, 1870, Capt. Sutherland has resided here all his life. His parents were Alexander and Margaret Sutherland, both belonging to old Kingston families. His father operated a custom shoe factory in Kingston. Capt. Sutherland is one of 11 children.

* * *

Capt. Sutherland received his education in Kingston public schools and the Dominion Business College. He became a bookkeeper in Muckleson's Hardware when he was 19 years of age. Not long afterwards he entered his father's business where he remained a short time. He and his brother John Henry still living in Kingston, operated the business for a time. Capt. Sutherland sold his interest and became a commercial shoe salesman, an occupation in which he spent more than 50 years.

His interest in hockey was apparent before it was officially recognized. He with other Kingston youths played on Kingston harbor. In 1886 he played with the Athletics, a newly formed Kingston league. Following the formation of the Ontario Hockey Association in 1890 Kingston teams enjoyed many s . He was elected president of the OHA in 1915 and the same year was chosen president of the newly formed Canadian Amateur Hockey Association. He remained as president of the OHA for two years and the CAHA for four years.

Capt. Sutherland was instrumental in the formation of the Hockey Hall of Fame which is to be built in Kingston. In 1947 the board of governors placed his name on the hall's honor roll as one of hockey's immortal builders.

Capt. Sutherland served with the Canadian Army overseas in World War I. He had previously served with the Canadian Reserve Army. Three months before the end of hostilities he was ordered to France and was in Paris when the armistice was signed. He returned to Canada in 1919.

* * *

Mrs. Sutherland, the former Ethel Mary Metcalfe, is a daughter of the late James H. Metcalfe, MP and MLA, and Mrs. Metcalfe. Her father was a school teacher by profession and was principal of Wellington, Louise and Queen street schools. He represented Kingston in the Ontario Legislature for eight years, and also a similar period in the House of Commons. He was later warden of the Kingston Penitentiary. Her forebearers were of United Empire stock.

Capt. Anita Margery, a daughter, wife of Dr E. S. McBride, Kingston, died in 1945. Capt. and Mrs. Sutherland speak of the death of Mrs. McBride as the tragedy of their lives.

Kingston's "elder statesman of hockey" died in 1955 just short of his 85th birthday. He was buried in historic Cataraqui Cemetery, not far from the grave of Canada's first Prime Minister, John A. Macdonald. A granite obelisk contains his captain title and the crest of the hockey shrine.

One of Sutherland's favourite professional players was Aubrey Victor (Dit)
Clapper, the first player to star in the league for 20 years. He proudly posed in
his No. 5 sweater on the steps of his Kingston home, 55 Sydenham Street,
with ancient hockey sticks.

UNDER FIRE AGAIN

(1956-1959)

1. ONE TOO MANY

In the mid-1950s, with the venerable hockey patriarch resting peacefully in his grave and the Hall of Fame flame barely flickering in Kingston, the hope for a permanent shrine was confused by rumblings out of Toronto. Harry I. Price, chairman of the CNE sports committee, who spearheaded the establishment of an all-embracing shrine for Canadian sports, offered space to the NHL for a hockey exhibit in a small room of the old administration building. Under this impetus, a group of prominent sports editors and writers from across Canada met in June 1955 and selected 55 members for the new Toronto sports shrine. They honoured ten more in 1956 and added three more in 1957 and six in 1958, but no additional hockey players.

"Though the initial displays were 'quite modest in nature' the building was a great source of interest to all who attended the Toronto exhibition," proclaimed the new Hall's initial brochure. While the NHL, CAHA, and the City of Toronto discussed plans for a new shrine, the Kingston group—stubbornly guarding the 'International" title and the monies and memorabilia donated to its long-delayed project—went doggedly ahead with its oft postponed plans and hopes.

Months later the Toronto group opened the doors wide open—and welcomed a new lineup of hockeyists.

The CNE-led Toronto group pressed ahead. When Canada' Sports Hall of Fame republished its modest 25-cent Souvenir Programme in the Fall of 1957, it contained a "National Hockey Hall of Fame" honour roll that listed 23 players and 10 builders previously inducted into the homeless Kingston shrine. It was a bit confusing as by March 1957, the International Hall advertised the 32 players and 10 builders as members in the Toronto Maple Leaf Gardens' program. No mention was made of the CNE project.

Months later the Toronto group opened the doors wide open—and welcomed a new lineup of hockeyists. A special insert in the sports hall of fame program provided thumbnail bios on seven new "Builders"—Donat

Raymond, James Norris, Lloyd Turner, George McNamara, Al Pickard, George Dudley, and—holder of seven Stanley Cups—Conn Smythe, plus 23 'Players,' including several previously inducted into the International Hockey Hall of Fame. Leading the more recently inducted players were Frank (King) Clancy, Frank Boucher, Ching Johnson, Dick Irvin and New York American player/manager Red Dutton, who was NHL president when the "Hockey Birthplace/Hall of Fame" debate started in the mid-1940s.

"A separate room is devoted exclusively to these hockey greats," the CNE advised. "Recorded are their pictures and their records of achievements … (and) most of the famous trophies which the hockey teams strive to win." At the same time as Toronto initiatives progressed, Kingston was still negotiating with the NHL. President Campbell agreed to visit the city and be interviewed by the mayor, chamber of commerce president, and three members of the Hall of Fame committee. "You will have observed, of course," he cautioned, "that we are presently engaged in some litigation which has to be my primary concern at the moment but it should not constitute too great a barrier to our meeting." The meeting came to naught.

By this time the strong supporters of the Kingston project were questioning its viability, if not throwing in the towel. With sadness, Mike Rodden reported that Boston's Art Ross, already inducted into the Kingston shrine, had "abandoned hope" the Hall would be erected in the Limestone City. He said the recently retired Bruins' mentor had openly wondered if lack of civic enterprise cost Kingston "this honoured place in a nation." Rodden said Ross could be excused for looking askance at what he termed "the alleged Hall of Fame" in Toronto. "He knows…that Toronto has no right whatever to occupy, even indirectly, such a lofty pedestal in the sun," said *The Whig-Standard* sports scribe. In a letter to Kingston shrine secretary St. Remy, Ross said "federal and provincial help was required to insure the success of your project." Kingston City Council took note but no aggressive resolution of support resulted. The Kingston bubble burst completely on January 11, 1959, when President Campbell issued a press release explaining that the NHL governors "had agreed to assist" the Canadian National Exhibition in establishing a hockey hall of fame at the exhibition grounds. The decision meant, he added, the International Hockey Hall of Fame (HHF) at Kingston would not be proceeded with, "at least not on as large a scale."

The final nail in the Kingston coffin was almost driven 18 days later when Campbell told Rex McLeod of *The Globe and Mail* that a permanent hall was "under consideration" for Toronto, subject to approval of the NHL board of governors. "The initial proposal wasn't quite satisfactory," said the NHL president. "A satisfactory site has been agreed upon for a new building and the cost has been discussed. But there are quite a number of details to be considered." The CNE's president Price was more optimistic: "We hope to have it ready by 1960 and keep it open all-year round."

Art Ross, already inducted into the Kingston shrine, had "abandoned hope" the Hall would be erected in the Limestone City.

Campbell explained that the current hockey exhibit space at the CNE didn't meet museum fireproof regulations. Six years earlier he had rejected a former United Church as the site of the Kingston hall. "Primarily such an institution is a museum for the safe-keeping of heirlooms of the game," he declared, "and to make a building fireproof would run into fantastic costs (estimated at $10,000) and would not be suited for accommodation of the public or the people responsible for running it."

The depleted Kingston committee had to scurry to look after housekeeping matters—mainly legal.

A local law firm pointed out that the IHHF had not held an annual meeting between 1951 and 1958 and urged members to do so in order to retain its provincial charter. The Toronto group made it known that they would like to acquire the "International" name. Ben Cunningham, a director and solicitor, told the 1959 Annual Meeting that the IHFM name could not be used by anyone else but the present incorporated body. "Funds (received by the Kingston organization)," he advised, "could not be used for any other purpose except for building of the shrine in Kingston or the vicinity."

"We decided," he said, "to build our own building even if we never put a hockey player in it—the way the NHL cut our throats!"

The day after the meeting IHHF President James Garvin announced to the press that plans to proceed with the building had been approved and architects Drever and Smith had proposed "a suitable memorial building" could be constructed with the available funds. "The site…will overlook the scene of where the first organized hockey was played in Canada." That is, Kingston Harbour in front of historic City Hall.

The latter statement referred to the fact that the Kingston committee had sought a building site at Old Fort Henry, a popular heritage site, located just east of the city in the historic hamlet of Barriefield or Pittsburgh Township. Word from officials in Ottawa indicated neither property nor grant funds would be forthcoming. The search for a site for Sutherland's dream shrine went on. The initiative could very well be tagged "The House of James." James the First was gone, but two others blessed with that moniker battled on—James Garvin, the president, and James de St. Remy, the secretary-treasurer. Holding no office but playing a prominent public relations role was Kingston businessman, benefactor, and former professional hockey player W.D. (Wally) Elmer, who had strong feelings about Sutherland's dream. "We decided," he said, "to build our own building even if we never put a hockey player in it—the way the NHL cut our throats!"

Sutherland was gone but not completely forgotten. In September 1959, the dynamo president of the CNE, Harry Price, issued a press release on behalf of the hall of fame organizing committee. He expressed a desire to meet with the Kingston people and hoped they would cooperate in a venture to recognize "in some appropriate fashion" the contribution made by late Captain

James T. Sutherland as 'founder' of the Hockey Hall of Fame and the City of Kingston as "the birthplace of hockey." The announcement coincided with a luncheon meeting in Toronto at which the NHL feted 31 of the 34 living members of the Hall, including three new inductees: Jack Adams of Detroit; Cecil (Tiny) Thompson of Edmonton; and Cyril (Cy) Denneny of Ottawa. The honorees were presented with crests, and three missing members—Donald Bain, Frank Patrick, and Senator Raymond— received theirs by mail.

"All in all it was a marvelous day for the grand old winter game of hockey," reported former *Toronto Telegram* columnist Bobby Hewitson, the newly appointed curator of the hall. Recording the historic event for the Maple Leaf Gardens' program, he concluded his report with the words of Grantland Rice's epic poem—*The Record*:

> When the game is done and players creep
> One by one to the League of Sleep…
> So take, my lad, what the Great Game gives
> For all men die—but the Record lives.

2. FOR THE RECORD

"The Record" of the trials and tribulations of creating a hockey shrine and honouring its greats was well under way. One of the first accounts of the founding of its initial home was recorded by Frank J. Selke, a member of the Toronto organizing committee in his 1962 book *Behind The Cheering*. Its board of directors included chairman Price, Clarence Campbell, Robert LeBel of the CAHA, and Conn Smythe of the Toronto Maple Leafs. Selke, then general manager of the Montreal Canadiens, gave full credit to Smythe, his former boss at Maple Leaf Gardens, for spearheading the Hall's move to Toronto and the erection of a permanent home on a choice CNE site. "He had an iron will, is a tough bargainer and a most able executive," he said.

Instead of $40,000 each for the original six NHL franchises, the NHL pledged $100,000 per team to cover all costs.

When Campbell set a figure of $240,000 for a building, Smythe told Selke to go ahead: "I'll see you get the money." He did. Instead of $40,000 each for the original six NHL franchises, the NHL pledged $100,000 per team to cover all costs, with maintenance provided by the City of Toronto through the Exhibition Board.

The first selection committee, according to Selke, was chaired by Lester Patrick and included: Cyclone Taylor, British Columbia; Red Dutton, Alberta; Al Pickard, Saskatchewan; Jim Dunn, Manitoba; George Dudley, Ontario, Milt Dunnell, Ontario; Basil O'Meara, Ottawa and English Quebec; Marcel Desjardins, French Canada, Danny Gallivan, Maritimes; and Walter A. Brown of Boston. It was this distinguished panel who were to come to the happy decision to honour the Hall's founder with induction as a builder.

As 1960 dawned, the hockey world was not exactly buzzing over the possibility of having a hall of fame, let alone two such shrines in Toronto and Kingston. Prime mover Frank Selke and two recently enshrined builders, Conn Smythe and Jack Adams and their teams, were battling it out for leadership of the NHL and reserving time to make the shrine become a reality.

Smythe's papers show that even during a visit to New York, he found time to review perspective sketches of the shrine at the CNE between the grandstand and the Pure Food building. Later in the year the Maple Leaf mogul reviewed a breakdown of costs totalling $487,000 for the building scheduled to open in 1961. "Avoid the words 'Canada" and 'International,"

he cautioned the architects, "both of which might be controversial."

At Kingston, where Hall of Fame survivors clung to the original "International" name, activity was stirred at a political level. In June 1960, City Council cited "the depletion by death of certain members" of the local committee and gave notice of a rescue mission. "Whereas the City of Kingston has a definite interest in this project as it will be located in this City which is rightfully known as the birthplace of hockey, as well as a financial interest through a donation of $5,000, for the purpose of constructing such a building: that Council request permission…to appoint three members of Council to the Committee."

The following month the IHHF Kingston committee—"an incorporated body"— passed a significant motion: "Whereas the late Capt. James T. Sutherland has proved without reasonable doubt that the first organized hockey game was played in Kingston, it is recommended that immediate action be taken to erect an IHHF in Kingston." The recommended building, near the decade-old Community Memorial Centre, would include a public auditorium with a hall of fame on the second floor and operation and management under the Centre board.

Both Kingston and Toronto shrines were alive in

name but still lacking a building and the supporters of one were not happy about the twin projects. The Ontario Hockey Association requested information on what progress had been made on the Kingston project. "It is the hope and wish of the Executive," wrote OHA business manager Bill Hanley, "that the venture be completed but quite naturally if the money is not to be put to the use for which it was designated they will seek its return." He apparently referred to the OHA's share of the $10,000 CAHA grant.

CAHA president J.M. (Jack) Roxborough followed up with another letter to the Kingston group. "It is the feeling…that more than ample time has been taken by your committee to do this work…and it is only fair that this money be now returned to the CAHA." Kingston Hall authorities remained silent and kept their purses tight. Concerned by the lack of a response, CAHA secretary-manager Gordon W. Juckes kept up the pressure in September 1960 and requested a meeting as soon as possible.

A month later, secretary-treasurer St. Remy responded and promised action when President Garvin, a keen baseball fan, returned from the World Series. He charged that the Kingston committee had been held up "by the attitude of the NHL" and specifically Clarence Campbell's refusal to okay a number of sites. The NHL president, he reported, would not approve funding for a building anything less than $250,000.

On September 9, 1960, in the midst of the dispute, one of the greatest of the great players and an early inductee—Fred (Cyclone) Taylor—turned the first sod for the Toronto hall.

On September 9, 1960, in the midst of the dispute, one of the greatest of the great players and an early inductee—Fred (Cyclone) Taylor—turned the first sod for the Toronto hall, with *Hockey Night in Canada* broadcaster Foster Hewitt at his side and honoured members applauding.

3. A GRAND PLACE

Despite the Toronto action, the original Kingston project had its supporters of note. T.P. (Tommy) Gorman, who managed two Stanley Cup winners, offered historical hockey photos that he had declined to donate to the Toronto hall. He also offered a firm opinion on the chosen site. "I felt that the Hall of Fame should be located at Kingston or Montreal," he said in October, 1960. "I disagreed with the Montreal men, who decided it should be operated as a sideshow for the Toronto National Exhibition, which it has become. I think they sold poor old Jim Sutherland 'down the river.'" He strongly recommended that Kingston Hall be located on Highway 401—where it would prove "a great attraction for tourists."

President Garvin and company also had to defend their procrastination on the home front. In 1960, Robert D. Owen, executive editor of *The Kingston Whig-Standard*, asked for facts and figures:

1. The total amount actually subscribed?
2. What portion (from) business concerns and industries?
3. How was the money from all sources invested?
4. What is the total amount of money earned?
5. In whose name...are the fund or investments registered?
6. Where are such funds...presently held?
7. Is an audited statement available?
8. Will it be made available in the near future?

Garvin conceded that the newspaper on behalf of the public was entitled to all the requested information, and referred Owen's letter to the treasurer and the auditors. Since the death of Captain Sutherland (five years earlier) the only disbursements, he advised, were minor charges for legal fees "and two wreaths to deceased members."

On another front, treasurer St. Remy replied positively to the OHA about the progress on the Kingston project, including news that the City of Kingston had placed $35,000 at their disposal, along with the original grant of $5,000. He also had to fend off a request from the distinguished Montreal sportsman William M. Northey, who had donated $1,000 and inquired about its use.

As construction plans proceeded on two fronts and the year waned (December 9, 1960), Montreal's Baz O'Meara—a member of both hall of fame boards—reported 51 honoured players in the Hall, headed by builders and cup donors, Lord Stanley and Sir Montagu Allan. "Of these, 26 are alive and 23 deceased," he recorded. "Among the 19 builders, eight are still alive."

In 1961, Kingstonians were greeted with a disturbing newspaper headline: "HOCKEY HALL OF FAME THREATENED BY LEGAL ACTION—CAHA Claims Kingston Group Held Secret Meetings." It was no surprise to the IHHF committee. Three months earlier,

Secretary-treasurer St. Remy had received a letter from Aurora lawyer T.A.M. (Ab) Hulse, acting on behalf of the Canadian Amateur Hockey Association, the United States Hockey Association, and the Ontario Hockey Association, seeking return of funds donated to the Kingston project. He demanded that no further plans be made for expenditures of the funds and asked for a definite commitment to meet with representatives of the three bodies. If a "definite undertaking" had not been made by November 17, 1960, Hulse said, "I will be forced to take the necessary legal steps to protect my clients' interests. I see no reason to add expense, or wash linen in public: the decision remains with your organization."

According to a Canadian Press story in early 1961, the CAHA maintained that the three associations had donated $40,000 for the Kingston Hall. (Actually, the total amount was $12,000 with $10,000 from the CAHA and $1,000 each from the USHA and OHA). "I don't suggest a copper has been misappropriated but Kingston has just ignored everybody," said lawyer Hulse, an OHA executive member.

President Garvin refuted Hulse's charges that the committee failed to keep others informed. "Meetings were held with no more secrecy that any board of directors of any company," he said. He issued a statement expressing regrets that the idea of the late Capt. James T. Sutherland "should now be questioned by the organization to which he gave too much of his life."

In June 1961, the largest class of modern players in the Hall's history was inducted. An impressive group of 14 was led by Maurice (Rocket) Richard.

The Toronto project continued to grow in stature. In June 1961, the largest class of modern players in the Hall's history was inducted. An impressive group of 14 was led by Maurice (Rocket) Richard, who had retired one year earlier and required a selection committee lifting of the five-year retirement ruling to qualify. Joining the Canadiens' great star were four former Toronto Maple Leafs: Syl Apps, Clarence (Happy) Day, Charlie Conacher, and George Hainsworth; Boston's Milt Schmidt; plus deceased old-timers Bruce Stuart, Percy Lesueur, Joe Hall, Frank Rankin, and Oliver Seibert. In the builder's category, Paul Loicq, the European who introduced hockey to the Olympics, plus American George V. Brown and pioneer Toronto referee Fred Waghorne were honoured.

Six weeks later, "The Fourteen" were formally inducted at the official opening of the Hall at the Canadian National Exhibition Grounds. With banners flying over the combined hockey and sports halls of fame, Prime Minister John Diefenbaker and United States Ambassador Livingston T. Merchant declared the $480,000 shrine officially opened. It was very much an NHL Hall, but the CAHA was granted a display of national trophies and space for listing meritorious award recipients.

Jim Sutherland originated the idea of a hockey hall of fame and it is a tragedy that nothing has been done about it in Kingston before he died...

At the same time in Kingston, specifications of labour and materials for the International Hockey Hall of Fame were reported by Kingston architects Drever and Smith. The directors signed an agreement with the city and contractor T.A. Andre & Sons to build a shrine with a 56 by 38 foot civic auditorium and a 24 by 38 foot stage on the first floor and a second floor displaying "historical hockey objects." Total cost, including a Winter Works grant: $131,905.

The two shrines, with a marked contrast in size and cost, drew national attention from Canadian Press sports editor Jack Sullivan in September 1961. "Sutherland nourished his dream," he wrote, "but Jim, a disillusioned 85-year-old died...and the only tangible sign of a hall was the bric-a-brac collection of sticks, skates and honour roll book he had stuffed under his four-poster bed and in the closets of his old home in Kingston." Sullivan opined that it was unlikely that the Kingston memorial would be recognized. "I think it is regrettable that there should be a conflict of this kind," commented NHL leader Campbell. "It is obvious that the Kingston hall will be very limited in scope and I don't know what the significance of being elected to it will be."

CAHA president Jack Roxborough rapped the two-hall concept. "Jim Sutherland originated the idea of a hockey hall of fame and it is a tragedy that nothing has been done about it in Kingston before he died...the Kingston people made no effort to build a hall until the Toronto site was proposed. Now, it is too late." President Garvin answered the criticisms. "There was no indicated change in the attitude of the NHL until Mr. Campbell's telephone call to myself that the governors had decided, if no further notice to us, to support the Toronto project.

"We have not criticized the Toronto project and do not feel that our original undertaking should be criticized," Garvin told *The Whig-Standard*. "We have the origin of organized hockey here in Kingston and the local founder of such...We have a sacred trust to the memory of James T. Sutherland and propose to carry out that trust in the erection of the International Hall at Kingston, Ontario, Canada."

On November 16, 1961, James A. Sutherland, son of the late founder, turned the first sod on city fairground's land at Alfred and York streets, adjacent to the Kingston Community Memorial Centre. "Construction is scheduled to start at once, ending 135 years of planning by local hockey enthusiasts," the Kingston's CP report read in Toronto's *Globe and Mail*. "But there is one catch—the Hockey Hall of Fame which opened last summer in Toronto is the one which hockey officials now recognize." "Full well might it be said" (about Sutherland's dream), chorused Mike Rodden in *The Whig*, "It is better late than never..."

FORT FRONTENAC, KINGSTON, ONTARIO

Ice hockey was first played by members of the Royal Canadian Rifles (an Imperial Unit) on the harbour in the rear of Tete-du-Pont barracks during the years of 1855 to 1869. It is also claimed that the military units played as early as the years 1846-1847. The old barracks originally built as Fort Frontenac in the year 1672 and converted into Tete-du-Pont military barracks in 1789 has been given its original name, and is now known officially as Fort Frontenac.

It has been claimed that Imperial troops stationed in Kingston as early as 1783 were proficient skaters and participated in field hockey, and very probably played field hockey on ice.

List of Candidates

Honoured by the Board of Governors

of

The International Hockey Hall of Fame

Prior to April 1st, 1953

COMPLIMENTS OF THE
INTERNATIONAL HOCKEY
HALL OF FAME
KINGSTON, ONTARIO

Captain Sutherland produced many pamphlets in support of his favourite project and made good use of historic buildings to illustrate Kingston's rich heritage. In a 1953 publication featuring the names of Hall of Fame inductees, he used a photo of Fort Frontenac, where British soldiers first played hockey.

As an *Official Guide for sports writers*, the following list of noted hockey men who are listed in *The International Hockey Hall of Fame "GOLDEN BOOK" at Kingston, is offered to sports writers as a helpful effort towards giving the men so selected the publicity that is theirs.*

The Officials of the Hall of Fame trust that this list will meet with your approval. The list will be added to from time to time as necessity requires. The names appear in the order in which the Candidates names were forwarded by the selecting Governors.

★ Howie Morenz
★ George Vezina
★ Frank McGee
★ Hobart Baker
★ C. R. "Chuck" Gardiner
★ Harvey Pulford
★ Eddie Gerard
★ Hod Stuart
★ Tom Phillips
★ John Ross Robertson
★ Frank Calder
Wm. A. Hewitt
Wm. M. Northey
★ Francis Nelson
Aubrey Victor Clapper
Lester Patrick
F. W. (Cyclone) Taylor
Edward Wm. Shore
Aurele Joliat

W. O. Cook

Frank Nighbor
★Allan "Scotty" Davidson
★ Capt. G. T. Richardson
Russel Bowie
Arthur Howey Ross
Donald M. Bain
★Chas. S. G. Drinkwater
Edouard Cyril LaLonde
★ Silas "Si" Griffis
Nels Stewart
R. R. "Dickie" Boon
Frank "Moose" Goheen
E. "Moose" Johnson
D. "Mickey" MacKay
Mike Grant
Joe Malone
Frank Patrick
Col. Harry Trihey
Capt. J. T. Sutherland

NOTE—*Recommendations for enrolment in the Hockey Hall of Fame should be addressed to President Clarence S. Campbell, Room 603, Sun Life Building, Montreal, Quebec, Chairman of the Selection Committee.*

★DECEASED

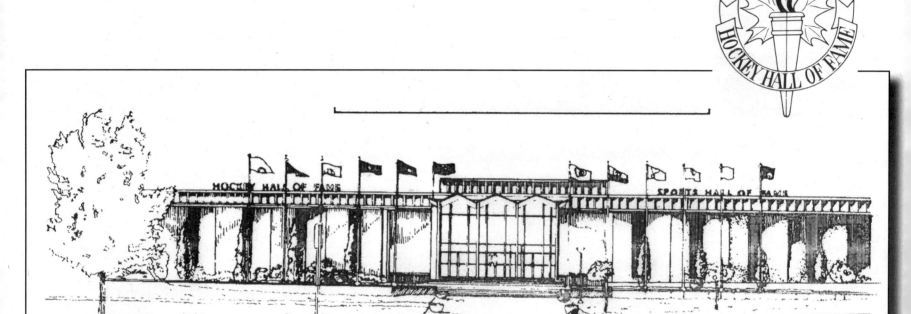

Leading the shift from Kingston to Toronto was Harry I. Price, chairman of the Canadian National Exhibition's Sports Committee. He worked tirelessly with NHL President Clarence Campbell to create Canada's Sports Hall of Fame, which included a separate hockey hall exhibit.

National Hockey Hall of Fame

The greats of ice hockey, Canada's national winter pastime, those who have made fame through their activity as players, and those who have given of their executive ability as founders and builders, are included in the National Hockey Hall of Fame.

Located at the Canadian National Exhibition in Toronto, as an important part of Canada's Sports Hall of Fame, the Hockey Hall, a separate room, is devoted exclusively to these hockey greats. Recorded are their pictures and their records of achievements.

Within the room for public view are most of the famous trophies, which the hockey teams, both pro and amateur, strive to win. Also on view are the trophies given for individual achievement.

Sweaters worn by some of the stars of the past, hockey sticks and hockey pucks that helped produce important goals are part of the most interesting display.

Established in 1957 the National Hockey Hall of Fame is the first time such a display has been set out for the general public to view.

National Hockey Hall of Fame 1957

- *Georges Vezina
- *Howie Morenz
- *Harvey Pulford
- *Eddie Gerard
- Frank McGee
- *Hod Stuart
- *Charles "Chuck" Gardiner
- *Tom Phillips
- Aubrey "Dit" Clapper
- Lester Patrick
- Frank Nighbor

- Edward William Shore
- Aurele Joliat
- Fred "Cyclone" Taylor
- Arthur H. Ross
- "Newsy" Lalonde
- Joe Malone
- *Allan "Scotty" Davidson
- *Silas "Si" Griffis
- Ernest "Moose" Johnson
- *Duncan "Mickey" MacKay
- William "Bill" Cook
- Nelson Stewart

Builders of Hockey

- *Lord Stanley of Preston, G.C.B.
- *Sir Montague Allan, C.V.O.
- *Frank Calder
- *John Ross Robertson
- William A. Hewitt

- *Francis Nelson
- William M. Northey
- Claude C. Robinson
- *Capt. James T. Sutherland
- Frank Patrick

*Deceased

10

Shortly after Captain Sutherland's death, Canada's Sports Hall of Fame opened at Toronto's Exhibition Grounds. Among the 55 inductees were three hockey players—Howie Morenz, Newsy Lalonde, and Canada's athlete of the half century, Lionel Conacher. The word "National" was dropped later and Kingston retained the "International" tag.

CANADA'S SPORTS HALL OF FAME

CANADIAN NATIONAL EXHIBITION

SOUVENIR PROGRAMME • PRICE 25 CENT[S]

1957

Shortly after the Toronto Hall opening, Kingston officials gathered at the fairgrounds to watch James Alexander Sutherland, son of the founder, turn the first sod, supported by Secretary-Treasurer James de St. Remy and President James B. Garvin—a "James hat trick!"

—Ross—Staff

SOD TURNING — Construction of Kingston's Hockey Hall of Fame got under way this morning after official sod turning ceremonies. On the shovel is J. A. Sutherland, son of the late Capt. James T. Sutherland to whom the hall is dedicated. With him is Magistrate James B. Garvin, head of the International Hockey Hall of Fame Inc. In centre background is James de St. Remy, treasurer.

The value of maintaining two hockey shrines was still being debated in 1989.

The Square Puck

THE OFFICIAL NEWSLETTER OF THE INTERNATIONAL HOCKEY HALL OF FAME AND MUSEUM, INC.

Kingston, Ontario, Canada

November, 1989

Vol. 1, No. 1

Why Two Halls Of Fame in Canada?

By Bill Fitsell

Forty-six years ago in September, 1943 - in the midst of the Second World War - many Kingston hockey buffs were jubilant. The National Hockey League and the Canadian Hockey Association had just announced the selection of Kingston as the site of the world's first Hockey Hall of Fame.

The local committee, which had conducted a year-long campaign for the honor, saw the proposed hall as a future tourist attraction. Then the howling began.

The protest came from Montreal and authorities which had joined Kingston in the debate over which city was the true birthplace of the game.

The Kingston group, inspired by the 1939 opening of the Baseball Hall of Fame in Cooperstown, N.Y., ignored the number of supporters and expanded their fund-raising campaign and started a building campaign. What followed was a most fluctuating post-war construction period marked by spiralling construction costs, lack of a suitable building site, competition from other charitable campaigns and buildings projects - foot-dragging by the NHL and a declining interest and action by the aging and procrastinating Board of Directors.

Bearing the brunt of the work on behalf of the International Hockey Hall of Fame in Kingston was Capt. James Thomas Sutherland, a well-travelled shoe salesman, who preferred to talk hockey on his cross Canada travels. He had devoted more than 50 of his 73 years to Canada's great winter sport and had used his close connections with the leading amateur and professional executives to swing the Hall of Fame award to his native city.

He was one of the first elected as a builder of hockey in 1947. The late Elmer Ferguson of the Montreal Herald - radio's Hot Stove League commented: "Cap'n Jim ... is the man responsible for the whole thing at Kingston, the man who for sheer love of the game has worked indefatigably to get the hall established. If anyone deserves a mythical niche in the hall which is mythical, to now, it's this venerable enthusiast."

This highly-respected life member of the NHL and the OHA, saluted as the "Poppa of Hockey" in Ontario, gathered other sporting honors which he would have gladly traded for his one major goal. His favored Hall of Fame project began to falter. Despite playing exhibition games in the old Jock Harty Arena and the Kingston principles making sorties to Boston, New York and Montreal to honor new inductees - Clapper, Shore, Ross, Patrick and Joliat - the project ran into down periods and defeats.

(continued on page 3)

Task Force Studying World's Original Hockey Shrine

A task force appointed by Mayor Helen Cooper to examine the operations of the International Hockey Hall of Fame and Museum has begun sittings.

The seven-member group, headed by Kingston lawyer Roy B. Conacher, met Oct. 24 with the Board of Directors of the Hall of Fame.

The mayor's task force was requested by the Hall's Board with the aim of improving community awareness and long-range operation of the shrine.

Mr. Conacher, son of the late National Hockey League star, Roy Conacher, said the task force will examine the operation "from stem to stern" and make recommendations on whether to leave it at its present location or move it perhaps closer to the tourist trail in the downtown location.

Located in the city-owned building near the Kingston Memorial Centre, the hall operates independently of the NHL and the Canadian Amateur Hockey Association, which originally sanctioned it in 1943. The building was opened in 1965, and honors the same members as the NHL-sponsored hall in Toronto.

"The Hall of Fame is a valuable asset for the city," Mr. Conacher told President Bill Crews and his fellow directors. "We plan to make a very detailed report and I hope the mayor and council take the recommendations seriously and act on them."

He indicated the task force might approach and consult with officials of other Halls of Fames, including the NHL-sponsored hockey shrine in Toronto and the Baseball Hall of Fame in Cooperstown, N.Y., which served as a model for the Kingston hall.

A report to mayor and council is expected early in 1990.

Task force members include Katherine (Cookie) Cartwright, Kingston lawyer and sports activist; Joseph Hawkins, a sportsman and former city alderman; Norm Saunders of Kingston Township, who has national and international hockey management experience and Michael Ross, of Mill and Ross Architects. Serving as special advisors are Douglas Fluhrer, Parks and Recreation Commissioner and Ronald Clark, Manager of Kingston Memorial Centre.

A MEMORABLE MEMORIAL

(1960-1970)

"We'll locate it in the city providing the best evidence that hockey originated there."-- *There's Nothing New In Sports*, **Hal Butler, 1964.**

1. OPENING CEREMONIES

Six years after the founder of the Hall of Fame movement went to his last reward, his hometown paper—*The Kingston Whig-Standard*—streamed a headline that would have pleased him greatly: "DREAM FULFILL-MENT DRAWS NEAR."

How true was the theme of this lengthy report on nearly two decades of "planning, fund-raising and organization problems" for a building slated to cost $133,000? Dated February 20, 1962, the story focused on details of the structure from the Queenston limestone entrance and terrazzo-floored foyer to the 250-seat auditorium with 30 by 16-foot stage and orchestra pit planned for use of theatrical, musical, and recreational groups. Not one word was stated about the hockey heroes it honoured, including its founder—Sutherland!

Ten months later, the same newspaper reported the new building was proving "a popular place" for several Kingston groups at rental rates ranging from $10 to $40. The anonymous writer confessed the building was several months away from fulfilling its function as a hockey shrine.

Local hockey fans suggested the Hall would not be able to fulfill its mandate because the Toronto shrine would receive mementoes and other displays from the NHL and CAHA "which have disowned Kingston's hall." Kingston's Leo LaFleur, the shrine's energetic executive director and chair of the Community Memorial Centre board, which controlled the hall, juggled limited finances to provide showcases and other equipment. The project was still a year away from receiving a special $10,000 grant from the City of Kingston to purchase furniture and equipment. "It's getting there," said LaFleur, estimating a January 1964 opening. Three months later, Kingston's one time chief booster—Clarence Campbell—toured the Hall, posed for pictures, but made no commitment from the NHL.

Finally, on July 29, 1965, Sutherland's dream of honouring his beloved game in his beloved hometown happened. The IHHF opened with little fanfare and a small notice that invited adults—at 25 cents a head—to see "Old Time hockey exhibits in the Birthplace of Hockey." Featured were Mike Rodden and the skates he wore refereeing hundreds of NHL games; an ornate Japanese vase received by a touring Battleford,

Saskatchewan team, and Dit Clapper's No. 5 Boston sweater, one of many mementoes collected by Capt. Sutherland. Also featured was a huge silver trophy dedicated to sportsmanship. Ironically it was never awarded to any sportsman and now languishes in a corner of the hall's boardroom.

Finally, on July 29, 1965, Sutherland's dream of honouring his beloved game in his beloved hometown happened. The IHHF opened with little fanfare.

It was not a gala affair—just local officials and sportsmen, including Augustus (Gus) Marker, Fred (Bun) Cook, George Patterson, and ex-Maple Leaf captain and future Hall of Famer Syl Apps, MPP for Kingston and the Islands. "I think it will go over big with the tourists," Jim McCormick, manager of the nearby Kingston Community Memorial Centre predicted. President Garvin added the most appropriate tribute: "If there's any one distinguished person responsible for this building, it's Captain James T. Sutherland."

Meanwhile, the Toronto Hall drew plaudits from The *Christian Science Monitor* published in Boston. An article headed "A Visit to Canada's 'Cooperstown'—a title Kingston coveted—extolled the CNE shrine as managed by R.W. (Bobby) Hewitson, a recently retired sports editor of the *Toronto Telegram*. "In August, during the annual exhibition, we attract thousands of visitors (free of charge)," the diminutive one-time NHL referee said proudly. "Our hours during the rest of the year are 2 to 4 p.m. every day—even on Sundays."

In addition to a 50 by 130 foot main exhibition room, the new structure housed an entrance concourse "with lush offices and control rooms," a mezzanine level with windowed gallery, and a 100-seat theatre showing 30-minute films daily. "Superb, freehand likenesses of each inducted member," not the photographs collected and framed by Capt. Sutherland, highlighted the gallery. The only concession to the original shrine were the words: "From a small beginning at Kingston, Ontario, today's growing Hall of Fame at Toronto is a grand, dignified showplace."

In June 1966, the Honour Roll of hockey heroes was graced by the man who had helped manoeuver the Kingston-Toronto switch. Clarence S. Campbell, selected as a builder, was saluted by the head of the selection committee, Frank J. Selke of Montreal. "Few men in the game's entire history have contributed more to hockey than has Mr. Campbell," he said. "His leadership, integrity and uncommon drive have been prime causes of hockey's growth to one of the world's most popular spectator sports."

Also saluted were other members of the 1966 class: Ted Lindsay, Ted Kennedy, Toe Blake, Elmer Lach, Babe Pratt, Max Bentley, Frank Brimsek, Butch Bouchard, and Ken Reardon. The selections demonstrated the power of the Montreal Canadiens and the influence of its general manager—Selke.

The establishment of two Halls of Fame and the reams of publicity over the annual inductions did not overshadow the hot debate over the game's beginnings. In fact, President Campbell entered the discussion. "The game of ice hockey did not exist until the first rules were drawn up and a game was played," he told Andy O'Brien author of *Headline Hockey* in 1965. "As such, ice hockey has to be regarded as strictly Canadian." However, O'Brien pointed out that no formal scientific research had ever been conducted on this issue.

At the same time the first scholarly evidence of the game's pioneer roots surfaced in a Nova Scotian city. Had it been discovered 20 years earlier, the place identified in wartime as "An Eastern Canadian Port," might have been chosen as hockey's birthplace. In June 1965, Nova Scotian archivist Charles Bruce Fergusson published an article—"Early Hockey at Halifax"—in the prestigious *Journal of Education*. In an academic manner, he documented the beginnings of a stick-ball game on ice in the early part of the 19th century. He recorded the playing of "the spirit-stirring games of wicket" and ricket on ice at Halifax-Dartmouth as early as 1831, well before any reported similar games at Montreal or Kingston. By 1859, rudimentary ricket rules could be ascertained from newspaper reports. "Any number can play this game, and generally, the 'more the merrier.'" said Fergusson. "Each ricketer is provided with a hurley…and a ball is thrown in the air…to commence play." By 1864 the game reports—with no mention of a puck—morphed into accounts of "hockey on the ice."

Henry Roxborough, one of the early Canadian sports historians, and author of *One Hundred—Not Out*, said Halifax might well be the source of pioneer hockey but with a caveat: "There is equally no doubt that Montreal, because of its experimenting, organizing, legislating, and developing is entitled to be recognized as the birthplace of modern hockey."

James Garvin, then in his 15th year as president of the Hockey Hall of Fame, had given fair warning that he was ready to hand the Kingston torch over to "a group of dynamic younger men," but hung on for one more kick at the can. In July 5, 1966, he stole a march on the new and invigorated Toronto shrine by announcing the acceptance of Fred J. (Bun) Cook and Harvey (Busher) Jackson as members of the International Hall at Kingston. Jackson was a member of the Leaf's famous Kid Line, while Cook played left wing on the bread line on another potent combination with brother Bill Cook and centre Frank Boucher. The surprising selections of Cook and Jackson were prompted by the prodding of former *Whig-Standard* sports editor Paul Rimstead, then with *The Globe and Mail*.

He stole a march on the new and invigorated Toronto shrine by announcing the acceptance of Fred J. (Bun) Cook and Harvey (Busher) Jackson as members of the International Hall at Kingston.

"It's wonderful to get in—I'm finally back with Bill," said Bun, an award-winning American Hockey League champion for 19 years. He told *The Whig* he was just as pleased with the honour for Jackson, who had a drinking problem in retirement. "What Busher did after he was through with hockey shouldn't matter." Five years later, the national shrine agreed and inducted the flashy Toronto left winger. It took much longer to accept Bun Cook. He made it into the NHL hall in 1995, on the recommendation of the Veterans' selection committee, an initiative since discontinued.

2. HOCKEY CENTRAL

In Canada's Centennial Year, the Kingston shrine became "hockey central" for the first Canadian-wide midget hockey tournament. Mr. Hockey, Gordie Howe, donated a pair of his brown leather hockey gloves that were sprayed with gold and silver paint and formed the championship and runners-up trophies. One of the many volunteers recruited to organize the 12-team competition was yours truly, then a middle-aged editor of *The Whig-Standard*, who saw the plight of the Hall of Fame and poured out his views in an opposite editorial page feature article entitled: "Hockey Hall of Fame—or hockey hall of shame?"

"If Captain Jim could look down from his gallery seat today he would no doubt shed a tear—for the Kingston shrine, for the game he loved so much is a far cry from what he must have envisioned and for which he collected and contributed many items," wrote yours truly. "It is an unwanted orphan, devoid of funds and lacking energetic leadership and enterprising promotion. It sits unheralded and without even a prominent sign, upstairs in a building that is better known as a site for dances, receptions, meetings and parties."

The article proposed a revitalization program with more emphasis on amateur and international hockey. It caught the attention of several Kingston citizens and sportsmen, including the surviving committee members. It also alerted the NHL's Clarence Campbell. M.H. (Lefty) Reid, who succeeded Hewitson as curator of the Toronto Hall, visited Kingston on his president's recommendation. The former *Toronto Telegram* sports writer inspected the Kingston shrine and the collection and took part in its successful Historic Hockey celebrations and apparently reported the shrine very much alive.

President Garvin turned over the president's gavel to Kingston businessman E.H. (Ebby) Hare, who had obtained for Kingston the extensive Tommy Gorman collection from Ottawa. *The Whig-Standard* editor, who had assessed the Hall's needs, took up the secretary and curator positions. The board of directors was strengthened by radio broadcaster Johnny Kelly, who made his name as a player, referee, and hockey tabloid publisher and BBC announcer in Scotland during the 1940s and early 1950s.

The new Kingston board members, struggling like their predecessors, ran into difficulties in 1970. Montreal Canadiens with Richard, Lach and company came to Kingston for an oldtimers' game but couldn't visit the original shrine. Apparently, the first floor public hall was double-booked for an event, and the Memorial Centre booking manager arranged to use the second floor Hall of Fame for the second event. When the mix-up hit the press, Magistrate Garvin was so incensed he threatened to issue a writ for a mandatory injunction to have the stored exhibits returned. Peace was restored but not before the embattled hall had been tagged by the local press as "A White Elephant."

3. NEW ERA

Five months later—in July 1970—the embarrassed shrine supporters were given a reprieve and a boost by the return of two Kingston players to their hometown. Rick Smith and Wayne Cashman, fresh from winning the Stanley Cup with the Boston Bruins, were greeted by an overflow crowd of vociferous fans who filled the first floor auditorium. "It was a smashing success," said President Hare. "We honoured two fine hockey players and hundreds of Kingston and area people saw our museum for the first time. It can't help but improve our project."

"We honoured two fine hockey players and hundreds of Kingston and area people saw our museum for the first time. It can't help but improve our project."

Strained for extra funds, the following year the directors sponsored Smockey Night, a fun night of games and races at the Memorial Centre. It attracted 1,313 fans, but like other fundraisers it was more a social than a financial success. The outreach program included assuming organization of the annual Historic Hockey Series that commemorates the first organized Kingston game between Queen's University and Royal Military College in 1886 and the Royal Canadian Horse Artillery regiments representing the soldiers who first played shinny on the harbour ice. This popular feature continues each February, not on the natural ice in front of Kingston's historic City Hall, but now on artificial ice of the Market Square—a "History Lesson on Ice." Seven players aside carrying short sticks chase a square puck under 19th century rules. A popular feature of the Kingston Winter Carnival, the round robin series for the RCHA Trophy attracted frost bitten crowds but added no funds to the Hall's coffers.

Gordie Howe loaned the International Hall a key exhibit—his No. 9 Houston Aeros sweater and the jerseys of sons Mark and Marty of the Houston Aeros.

Back at the Hall other lessons were offered through school class tours, which boosted 1972 visitor totals to a reported 4,000. The next year, Kingston celebrated its "Tercentennary" and players of eleven championship hockey teams from 1931 to 1968 were feted at a reception. The Hall honoured Ottawa 67's star forward Peter Lee, who presented his sweater, but little was received or accomplished on the professional front. That is until the World Hockey Association was formed and shunned by the NHL in 1972.

Gordie Howe loaned the International Hall a key exhibit—his No. 9 Houston Aeros sweater and the jerseys of sons Mark and Marty of the Houston Aeros. The family troika still remains a popular attraction. Later, Bobby Hull, another WHA star, pulled his memorabilia from the Toronto Hall and loaned it to Kingston. One key reason, he did not like that the NHL supported the Hall by charging admissions.

The first sports Hall to be recognized by the Province of Ontario for grant purposes, thanks to the urging of local MPP Syl Apps, the Kingston shrine became "The International Hockey Hall of Fame AND MUSEUM." The Hall and went from little strengths to little strengths. A major breakthrough came in 1978 when 13 directors signed a bank loan for $13,000. This provided a nest egg for a "Double Your Dollar" drive and the impetus to take over the complete two-storey, 7,000 square foot building and provide more colourful exhibits.

Clarence Campbell and Frank J. Selke accepted a long-standing invitation and applauded the Kingston accomplishment before an impressive guest list, including Hall of Famers Syl Apps, Bill Cook, Aurel Joliat, and a budding new NHL coach, Don Cherry. Speaking within a few blocks of the home that he left at age 15, "Grapes" paid tribute to the on-ice greats but reserved special commendation for Kingston's venerable hockey hero.

"Everyone knows Captain Sutherland was 'The Father of Hockey,'" said Cherry, the future host of the popular television program, *Hockey Night in Canada's Coach's Corner*. "This will tell you how much he was ahead of his time. In 1910, he advocated rubber goal posts. In all my years—I've played 18 seasons—I think goal posts right now are the most deadly things we have on the ice. It's much more sensible to do something about that than helmets."

"Everyone knows Captain Sutherland was 'The Father of Hockey,'" said Cherry, the future host of the popular television program, **Hockey Night in Canada's Coach's Corner.**

Cherry, then 43, and in his fourth successful season as coach of the Boston Bruins, seized the opportunity to pay tribute to the former NHL president, who, he said, had a one word answer—"Unacceptable" — for some of his unusual antics and coaching actions. "He's a wonderful man. There's nobody in hockey today more respected."

After Messrs. Campbell and Selke performed joint ribbon-cutting honours, they joined others guests for the dedication of the "Capt. James T. Sutherland Room" on the second floor. It was graced by a full-length, tinted photograph of a distinguished officer in uniform, whose countenance looked down as a tearful Mr. Campbell paid tribute to the founder. Hall President E.H. (Ebby) Hare, a justice of the peace, read a prayer of dedication prepared by the rector of Sutherland's St. Paul's Church: "May the qualities which he exemplified, his zeal, dedication, sportsmanship, his care and concern for others, be the heritage which you give to us who meet this day to honour him. We give thanks that you have given us the gift of play and ask that this room which we dedicate to the honour of your servant may always remind us that our lives are given to you to be used for your glory and the service of all men and His way."

Sutherland was gone but he was well remembered and saluted by loyal friends. Leading the way was Mike Rodden, a frail 82-year old whose mind burned brightly about the past. When the City of Kingston celebrated its Tercentenary in 1973 and the IHHFM published Rodden's old manuscript, "Kingston's Record Down the Winding Years," he paid tribute to the memory of Jim Sutherland, "a man of destiny," who served his country so well in war and his city so loyally in hockey. "Only those who knew Mr. Sutherland well knew about the vast amount of time he spent in tracing hockey's history," he wrote. "His was a very difficult task and it was tragedy that he did not live to see the fulfillment of his dreams (the erection of the IHHF) in this city. His researches were costly to himself but he never complained."

The International Hockey Hall of Fame finally opened in July 1965 with little fanfare. The top storey housed the exhibits, while the first floor was rented for civic functions.

Michael J. Rodden inspects somewhat sadly the skates he used to wind up his distinguished career as referee in the NHL and OHA. The well-taped boots and tubes were one of the first new donations made to the Kingston hall.

The Bread Line was united at the Original Hockey Hall of Fame. The Cooke brothers, Bill and Bun, centred by Frank Boucher, led the New York Rangers to victory in two Stanley Cups and led the league in scoring as a line for many years. The Hall of Fame has become a centre for various hockey events.

Rick Smith (left) and Wayne Cashman, (far right) two Kingston natives, won the Stanley Cup with the 1970 Boston Bruins. They were saluted at a big reception at the Kingston hall. Sharing the moment were Major Danny McLeod, noted Kingston coach, and sportscaster Ted Darling, then with the Buffalo Sabres.

Gordie Howe, who loaned his Houston WHA jersey to the Kingston shrine, was a big attraction at a reception in 1976. The former Detroit Red Wing star, despite arthritic wrists, never stopped signing until the last lad had his souvenir.

*The Golden Jet officially unveiled his collection at the Original
Hockey Hall of Fame in 1990.*

Jean Beliveau displayed his memorabilia in the showcases at the Original Hockey Hall of Fame while signing hundreds of autographs.

"I want to tell you what a wonderful per-
son, sportsman and booster for hockey Capt.
Sutherland was." – NHL President Clarence
Campbell

CAPTAIN SUTHERLAND'S LEGACY

1. SUTHERLAND'S ACHIEVEMENTS

The definitive biography of Captain James Thomas Sutherland—like the ultimate history of hockey's origin—has yet to be written.

From that first time when he played hockey on the ice in the Kingston harbour, James Sutherland stickhandled his way through all opposition. He lived the game, breathed it, and spoke it—with avuncular passion. There was no doubt that his love of hockey was ingrained in his spirit. He was an innovator who thought-outside-the-boards, particularly in safety matters. He campaigned for "clean sport, campaigned for universal rules." In the 1930s, he recommended teams carry a second goaltender and called for an end to bodychecking among junior and intermediate clubs. When players suffered injuries in crashing the net, he suggested the goal posts be covered in rubber He successfully advocated the naming of player positions and in the age of two 30-minute periods advocated shorter periods for under-20 juniors. As a rabid supporter of amateur hockey, he campaigned for the right of a man to earn a living playing hockey and favoured the reinstatement of former professional players who wanted to return to the simon pure game. The crowning achievement of this hockey soldier was to establish a memorial cup to commemorate Canada's First World War dead.

The same newspaper's venerable columnist, Mike Rodden, called Sutherland "hockey's first ambassador of goodwill." He spread its gospel far and wide.

Even in Sutherland's sunset years, this astute businessman, who spent a half-century selling shoes, put the memory of the game ahead of his main livelihood. In the sunset of his life in the 1950s, he took a noted leather company's album of samples, removed the bright, medium, and dull strips of brown calf and domestic thistle and highland grain he had used as a salesman and replaced them with newspaper clippings and other hockey ephemera highlighting his life.

What was the mark of the man called "The Grand Old Sports General" and "Poppa of Hockey?"

Observers vary in their opinions but most comments were ultra positive. In 1947, when Sutherland was elected to the Hall of Fame he helped create, Robert D. Owen, managing editor of _The Whig-Standard_ and son of a Primate of the Anglican Church of Canada, described him as "a big, affable man." That he was—and much more! The same newspaper's venerable columnist, Mike Rodden, called Sutherland "hockey's first ambassador of goodwill." He spread its gospel far and wide.

Above all, he was loyal—a faithful servant to Crown and Country through the Victorian, Edwardian, and Georgian eras and the start of the Elizabethan reign. He wore the symbol of monarchs on his cap badge. He revered "those who served with distinction." He coveted a royal salute and was recommended for an Order of the British Empire.

Other accolades and adjectives followed: one noted his "indomitable spirit and energy." As Kingston entered the new millennium in 2000, a contemporary writer profiled Sutherland as "a large, gregarious man with sparkling blue eyes." His official Hall of Fame citation linked him to men "who by their outstanding ability and deportment have placed the game of hockey on its present high pinnacle in the sport world." He was a true amateur—"a John Ross

Robertson amateur" in his words—but he admired professionals who strove for excellence and were rewarded in kind.

For a non-hockey perspective, we have the viewpoint of his closest living relative. "Grandfather was both generous and sentimental," said granddaughter Joan Sutherland Rippel. "He was a true Scotsman but loved to orate (even at family Christmas dinners)." One of her fondest early recollections of him was sitting on a hammock swing on the font porch of the Sutherland summer cottage at Amherst Island, west of Kingston, reciting "Jack and the Beanstalk."

Elmer Ferguson, a genial and highly respected columnist in Montreal, cited Sutherland as "enthusiastic" and "indefatigable." Without a doubt he was dedicated, resolute, and focused—almost to a fault. He was unbending in his support of Kingston as the one and only birthplace of hockey. In today's language he might be described as a denialist. Why did he take such a rigid stand in the face of evidence to the contrary? Undoubtedly, his origin beliefs were deeply entrenched—based on his own experience as a youth and the tales he heard from British soldiers in Kingston. He reluctantly acquiesced on Halifax and Montreal claims, giving them minor consideration and space in his final Origins report to the CAHA, but in the end he held true to his hometown.

Former NHL President Clarence Campbell highly praised his old friend in 1978 when he dedicated the Sutherland Room in the new and enlarged International Hockey Hall of Fame and Museum. "I want to tell you what a wonderful person, sportsman and booster for hockey Capt. Sutherland was," he said. "I shared with him and others, the hope and expectation that the Hockey Hall of Fame would be established in the birthplace of hockey. Unhappily, a number of developments occurred to prevent that dream becoming a possible fulfillment."

In 1983, Campbell revised his opinion of Sutherland's role in the long and fractious birthplace debate in a letter to yours truly. "The search for the real origin of the game was complicated enormously by the missionary efforts of the late Capt. James Sutherland," he wrote. "On every possible occasion he proclaimed that 'hockey' had its origin in Kingston, Ontario and eventually he persuaded the CAHA to declare Kingston to be 'the central site upon which to erect a shrine' dedicated to the greats of the game." Neither the Kingston nor the Toronto Hall of Fame developments, Campbell declared "really resolved the question of what was the true, original site of the game of 'hockey' during the next 20 years."

2. SUTHERLAND LIVES

At the outset of the new millennium little has changed. The NHL-supported Toronto hall continues to preserve the game's history in grand style at its third location—in downtown Toronto—while the original shrine struggles on in its only location in its 50-year history—in mid-Kingston—and strives to move to the tourist trail downtown.

Under the slogan "Honouring Our Best," the Kingston and District Sports Hall of Fame inducted 133 players and builders before remembering the man behind Canada's original hockey shrine. The honour came May 4, 2012—57 years after his death but with glowing praise from the Hockey Hall of Fame website: "His passion for the game inspired him to become the most creative and diligent administrator ever associated with hockey."

Another truth remains. This born and bred Kingstonian, well remembered at home but almost forgotten elsewhere, retains the title of "founder"— Toronto Hall officials were reluctant to attach that honour. However, in the glossy coffee table book, *Honoured Members*, published in 2003, an anonymous author conceded "he was the sole driving force in trying to establish a Hockey Hall of Fame to house artifacts and memories of the games great stars." The dust jacket confirmed the salute to the man who started collecting hockey memorabilia in 1910: "It was his vision that started what today is the greatest repository of hockey history in the world."

"It was his vision that started what today is the greatest repository of hockey history in the world."

Hockey lovers everywhere owe a debt of gratitude to this remarkable man. As actor and blues lover Hugh Lawrie proclaimed over the PBS network in 2012: ""Everyone is standing on the shoulders of giants." James Thomas Sutherland was a gentle giant who gave Canada's game a solid foundation by establishing a national memorial.

"Founder" is as solid and deserved an honourable title as the rank of Captain, which Sutherland carried to his grave. To me, he will always be "Hockey's Captain." In his home city, where hockey's roots run deep, this proud pioneer created a simple concept to honour the excellence of others, nurtured it through seven decades, and left a lasting legacy to Canada and its national game. He rests with pride!

SUTHERLAND LIVES

Forty-two years after his death in 1955, Captain Sutherland still lives in the minds of hockey aficionados. Videographer Dale Morrisey, a former assistant curator of the Kingston shrine, produced a documentary on his life in 2012, the same year the Captain was posthumously inducted into the Kingston and District Sports Hall of Fame. Present were his granddaughter Joan and grandson Brock Dew.

*Capt. Sutherland's daughter, Ethel May Dew, and son, James A. Sutherland,
inspect an honoured exhibit at the Sutherland Memorial Room, dedicated in 1978.
The exhibit includes Sutherland's personal effects.*

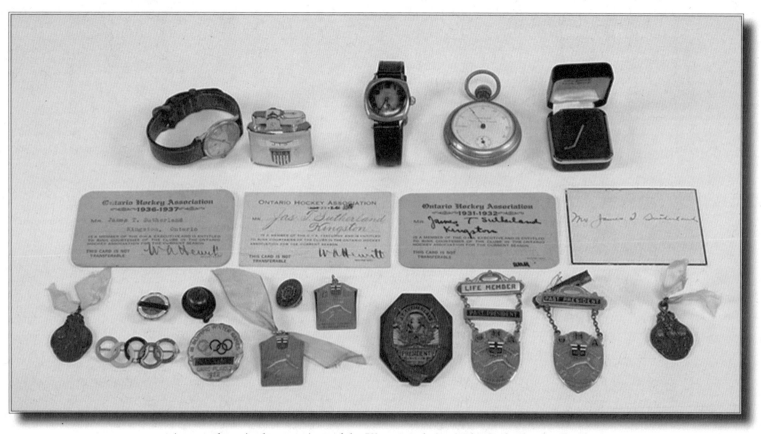

*Among the prized possessions of the Kingston shrine is the Sutherland collection
of medals and memorabilia from the Captain's 70-year career.
Note the OHA Gold Stick award (upper right) and 1932 Olympic pin (lower left).*

3. THE NEW ORIGINAL HOCKEY HALL OF FAME

Since the founding of the International Hockey Hall of Fame and Museum, Captain Sutherland's shrine has not thrived. Not even the founder could have imagined a more stormy existence. In the 1990s, despite the valiant efforts of Roy B. Conacher, son of Hall of Hall of Famer Roy Conacher, and the support of the International Ice Hockey Federation president Guenther Sabetzki, the Kingston directors failed to complete a long-lasting agreement to sustain a true International Hockey Museum. Despite a $100,000 line of credit from the City of Kingston and donations of IIHF artifacts from Europe, this dream fizzled and died, and the IIHF, under new president Rene Fasel, abandoned the cause.

Director Mark Potter, a well-known sportscaster, stepped into the breach as president and led a revival plan to relocate the Kingston Hall from its Memorial Centre property in mid-town to a site where the shrine could take advantage of the thousands of townsfolk and tourists in the thriving downtown business and entertainment section. The prize location was the recently restored S&R (Smith and Robinson) department store, an imposing, three-storey limestone structure, located a block away from City Hall, and the site of the first organized hockey game in Kingston, and a slapshot away from the K-Rock Centre, home of the Major Junior A Kingston Frontenacs.

The proposed move could not have come at a better time. The City of Kingston had all but condemned the original Hall because of mold and insulation problems, recommending that the 46-year-old building be demolished. Against these black clouds, reminiscent of hazards and hurdles faced in Sutherland's days, Potter, supported by loyal lieutenants Larry Paquette and Sy Golosky, created a ray of sunshine. They organized a fund-raising banquet featuring Kingston's favourite hockey son, Don Cherry, side-kick Ron MacLean, buddy Brian Kilrea, and general manager Doug Gilmour and coach Todd Gill of the Frontenacs, the name Sutherland had established more than a century ago.

The sold-out event raised $40,000 to kick off a $1.2 million drive to establish a state-of-the-art exhibit hall, museum, and research centre under the title of "Original Hockey Hall of Fame." Kingston aligned itself with the NHL-sponsored Toronto hall. Then came a request to Kingston City Council for a $400,000 grant, with the hope that it would be matched by provincial and federal governments. Despite vigorous lobbying and intense debate, City Council in a split vote put a damper on the move by cutting the grant amount to $200,000 and adding a rider that required the full financial goal be realized or no funds.

President Potter, using his media expertise, kept the Hall of Fame debate going on TV newscasts and on the front pages of the local press. Voicing the spirit of Sutherland, he told *The Whig-Standard*: "We have one of the best hockey collections in the world and I think it's time that we really showcased that collection."

Despite the brave front, Potter and company finally stepped away from the lease agreement on the S & R property that would have provided a prime location but only half of the 8,000 square feet in the original hall. Two other prospective sites were offered to the board, but with pressure mounting to abandon the original site, the City stepped in and offered 1,400 square feet, rent-free, in the new four-pad arena called the Invista Centre. The arena is located in the city's west-end, far from the preferred downtown site, but it provides a stop-gap measure for a two- to four-year period. The harried directors reluctantly accepted.

Miraculously, in the dog days of summer of 2012, the largest single donation ever made in the history of the Kingston shrine was joyfully announced by President Potter. The money came, not from a hockey enthusiast, but from the estate of a fervent baseball fan, W.J. (Bill) Henderson. The amount of the bequest was a surprising $250,000—more than totalling all other funds given to the project. A one-time director of the shrine and a Member of Parliament, "Judge" Henderson supported Sutherland's dream as he developed the Amherstview subdivision west of Kingston and served as a Justice of the Supreme Court of Canada. This magnanimous contribution could be the corner stone for a successful fundraising campaign. Appropriately, it came from an aficionado of a sport that inspired the establishment of his hockey shrine.

"Many people said a hall of fame would never be built in Kingston," Mark Potter reflected." Once it was built they said it would never survive. We've proved people wrong all along. After an interim move, we are going to relocate in the downtown and create a modern memorial of which Captain Sutherland would be justly proud."

Author Bill Fitsell points out new research discoveries displayed in the Sutherland Room to NHL President Clarence Campbell. The Sutherland Room was opened in 1978. Fitsell is co-founder of the Society for International Hockey Research (SIHR), which boasts more than 500 members worldwide.

THE ORIGINAL HOCKEY HALL OF FAME

IS ON THE MOVE

*An architectural rendering of a possible exterior
and exhibit showcase for a new Original Hockey Hall of Fame.*

The inimitable Don Cherry, Kingston's number one booster, seldom fails to acknowledge the achievement of great Kingstonians, including Captain Sutherland.